C++ and Python Programming 2 Bundle Manuscript

Introductory Beginners Guide to Learn C++ Programming and Python Programming

Series: Hacking Freedom and Data Driven (Junior Edition) & C++

By Isaac D. Cody

C++ PROGRAMMING & PYTHON PROGRAMMING

2 BUNDLE MANUSCRIPT

Introductory Beginners Guide to Learn C++
Programming and Python Programming

ISAAC D. CODY

QUICK TABLE OF CONTENTS

This book will contain 2 manuscripts from the Hacking Freedom and Data Driven series. It will essentially be two books into one.

The first part of this book will dive into learning the sophisticated programming language of C++ and get you on your way to program like a boss!

Hacking University: Junior Edition will introduce and enhance your Python programming skills from beginner to pro!

C++: Learn C++ Like a Boss

A Beginners Guide in Coding Programming And Dominating C++. Novice to Expert Guide To Learn and Master C++ Fast

By: Isaac D. Cody

C++

LEARN C++ LIKE A BOSS

A BEGINNERS GUIDE IN CODING PROGRAMMING AND DOMINATING C++

Novice to expert guide to learn
and master C++ FAST

ISAAC D. CODY

within this book are for clarifying purposes only and are the owned by the owners themselves, not affiliated with this document.

Table of Contents

Chapter 1: Basic Background, History, and the Fruition of C++

Before we get into how to start using C++, you have to learn what it is, and how it came about. The reason for this is simple. To truly know something, you have to know everything you possibly can learn about the subject, especially when it comes to something so technical such as computer programming.

C++ is a very important part of computer and Internet history. It is simply something that is interwoven within the history of the technological world, as we know today. Furthermore, the apps and other functions on a smart phone would not exist if it were not for C++.

When you are learning C++, you will be filled with wonder at the fact that one programming language can have so much impact in our daily lives. Almost every computer ever built can be attributed to a specific aspect that can be traced back to the language of C++. One of the benefits of learning this language is the ability to learn other languages with ease. Having the ability of learning C++ will enhance your knowledge of other programming language, which is why many people regard it as the 'godfather' of computer programming. Furthermore, many big companies still need programmers that have C++ as they rely this programming language to run their central computer system. So when the going gets tough, just know it'll benefit you in the long run so stay strong and get in the programming mindset!

History of C++

Bjarne Strousup was working on his thesis for his doctorate, and he decided to work with a programming language that was known as Simula. This language one one of the first programming languages of the computer age. However it was very slow and full of bugs.

Strousup came up with the idea of C with Classes. A programming language that was a lot faster than Simula. C with classes later became Cfront which sped up the process of creating a language. However, Cfront was left in the dust when C++ came along, because it added compilers into the language, making it a lot easier, and faster to use than any other project language of the time.

Since then there have been annotated reference guides and updates to the language to make it better and faster, and even easier to use. C++ for Dummies is a popular guide for this language.

C++ is one of the most popular languages out there today. This language is the best for many industries, so rather than make a new language which takes a lot of time, they just adapt C++ to many different variations because it is versatile in its nature.

Exactly what is C++

C++ is not just any programming language, it is object oriented. Object oriented programming or OOP for short, is programming that revolves around objects rather than actions. It is like looking at the whole picture at once, rather than each individual puzzle piece.

This programming language was designed with flexibility and speed in mind, as other languages of the time were way too slow, and could only do one thing, so every time you wanted to create something new, you needed a new language.

There are many things that you can use this language for, and they are still very much popular today, despite the ominous amount of languages that are out there now.

- Prepackaged scripts: These are what script enthusiasts, and new hackers use to practice their programming techniques. Since so many people nowadays want to take the easy way out, scripts that come already prepared are what most hackers are looking for, thus the packages need to improve, and they do so using C++.

- Video Games: Let's face it, pretty much everyone plays video games at some point in their life. Whether it is growing up, or when you have kids, you will get sucked into the realm of video games, and you can never escape. Those games can be attributed to some way or form from using the C++ language. If you are into making games, and bringing the world joy through graphics, then it is definitely a good idea to learn the language of C++

- Web pages: A lot of web pages are made using C++. The reason for this is because the language is so easy to manipulate, it makes for a quick and easy website that has plenty of interactive features for people. Some websites you may visit often that are created with C++ are Amazon and Ebay. If you like designing web pages you should learn C++ to be efficient and maybe even land a decent job in this field.

- Phone Apps: Nowadays it seems everyone has a smart phone, and that means apps galore. There are thousands of apps out there, and more are being made every day. Some apps are free, some apps cost money, but a good chunk were made using C++. That is because this language is so scalable that it can be used for simple games and more intricate shopping apps.

There are a lot of other minor things that C++ is used for, such as VoIP calling. That was created using C++. The fact of the matter is, you will get told time and time again that C++ is a dying language when in reality that is just a ruse that JAVA people uses to scare people into switching languages to ensure that C++ is a dying language.

Why It's used

C++ is used not only for its flexibility and speed, but because it has a lot of components, it is fairly easy to learn, and if you master C++, you can master the other languages with ease. The reason for this is that when you learn something that is a little more complex than everything else first, the easier stuff will fall right into place, however, if you get used to easy to learn subjects, then you will find that the more difficult stuff is hard to learn because you are not used to putting in that much effort into the subject that you are trying to learn.

If you want to learn a language that you can use for different types of functions within the realm of computer technology, then this is the language for you. You can do almost anything with it, and once you learn enough about it, you may be able to figure out ways to manipulate the language to do things that it generally cannot do.

C++ is a very important language when it comes to computer programming, and though it has a lot of variables from the way that it is laid out, it is very easy to read, and very easy to create. This makes it one of the most desired programming languages that are out there, because no one wants to struggle to read code. No one wants to have to spend all of their time out there working on what they know is right just because they cannot find where they went wrong.

Job Outlook

Yes, there are a lot of jobs out there that still rely on C++ to operate. There are so many different things that you could do, and all of them affect other people in the community. Video game designing, and web page designing are two of the most prominent things that are out there. You could also become a white hat or blue hat hacker.

But according to payscale.com (search software engineer), a person with C++ Software engineer background can earn up to $57,000 to $120,000 based on experience. The median is around $80,363. Some other titles that people with C++ programming language have is Computer Programmer, Electrical Engineer, and Application Developer.

However, to be the best that you can be, you should always know two or three programming languages to be marketable. Though those languages will not be included in this book, do not marry yourself to a single language. Instead, just like with human language, broaden your horizons and dabble in a few, but keep one as your main language.

C++ should be the main language that you fall back on due to its versatility. Maybe use JAVA or Linux as your other languages, but C++ is the best main language to have, and you only want the best as your main.

C++ is a statically written lower level language which means that it is a clean cut expansive language.

C++ is a fully functional super set of C that supports object oriented programming. This means that it supports all the pillars of OOP, such as encapsulation, data hiding, inheritance and polymorphism.

To learn more about object oriented programming, you can do a quick search online, and find out more about it. It is best to get some knowledge about what it is, but it is not quintessential to your knowledge of C++, so it will not really be included in this book, except for a few mentions in passing, and some tidbits of information here and there.

Three Important Components of C++

The standard C++ is made up of three very important concepts.

- Core Language: This is made up of all the variables, data types, literals, and other important aspects of the language, creating building blocks to get to the next level

- C++ Standard Library: this allows you to manipulate files, and other workings within the language, and bend them to your will.

- STL: This stands for Standard Template Library, which gives you functions to manipulate data structures and variables and other things of the sort.

Why is C++ considered the best language out there?

Well, aside from the copiously mentioned flexibility, speed, and simplicity, it is a language that has spanned over thirty years, and is still widely used today. There are not many products in any genre of life out there that can say the same. Products and companies come and go, but only true perfection stays. Well that is how the saying goes. To be honest, C++ has had many updates since then, but the core process is still the same. When it came out it was light years ahead of its time, and today it is still a pretty advanced piece of technology, due to the updates that keep it on top.

There are a lot of opinions that also have to do with why C++ is considered the best. While there are a lot of people who say that C++ is no longer relevant, even more vouch that it is still the best language out there, and it is their fall back language. It is the one they know the most about, and the one they carry close to their heart. The reasons vary, but the fact that 90% of programmers default to C++ shows that it is very much the best programming language out there today.

C++ is one of the few languages that follow the ANSI standard completely, which is why some of the best games you will ever play are still written with C++. Because their compilers are set to ensure that all commands are written and executed without errors. It can also be used across many different types of platforms, whether you have a Microsoft, Unix, Mac, Windows, or and Alpha device, it is possible to use C++. This is a great thing, because a lot of programmers have to operate across many different platforms, and the universality makes it easy and portable. Just throw your code on a flash drive and upload it wherever it is needed.

Benefits of using the C++ language

There are a lot of benefits that you will be able to enjoy when using the C++ language. Some of these benefits include:

- The big library: since C++ has been around for along time, they have a library that is pretty large. This is available for you to use so you can pick out the codes that you want inside of your script and save some time and even learn some new things. You can also create some of your own codes if you wish, but this library can be really helpful for the beginner who is learning and can make it easier than ever to get the code written.

- Ability to work with other languages: C++ is a great language to use with some of the other programming languages out there. This makes it easier to really work on the projects that you want because you can add in the parts that you like from different coding languages and combine them together to get something really amazing.

- Works on many projects: most other programming languages are going to focus on just one or two little projects. For example, using JavaScript means that you are just going to be working on websites. But with C++, you are able to use it to help with a lot of different projects. Whether you are looking to work on a website, looking to create a new program, or do something else with programming, you will be able to do it with the help of C++.

- Fast and reliable: if you have used some of the other coding languages that are popular in the past, you will find that sometimes they aren't the most reliable. Information may slip through or they won't start working the way that you would like. If you want something that works the first time and is reliable, then it is a good idea to go with C++.

- Offers a lot of power: those who like to work in programming and want to have a lot of power in the work that they are doing will find that C++ is the right option for them to choose. It has some of the best power for the programming languages that are out there.

These are just a few of the benefit that you can enjoy when you are using the C++ programming language. It may seem a bit more difficult to use than some of the others, such as Python, but it has a lot of the power that you need and can work well with other programming languages. With a bit of practice, you are going to get all the basics of this language down and really enjoy what you are able to do with this programming language.

Chapter 2: Let's Begin

Let's begin! There are a lot of places we can start, but let's talk about environments first. While you do not really need to set up your own environment, as there are many online. An environment is a compiler of your choice that takes your code, and does all of the functions for you. In the old days, you would have to open your command prompts and create an environment to use, but those days are over. A simple mistake back in the day could do some serious damage to their computers. Now you can practice some risky prompts without any risk to your device whatsoever.

There are many examples to try out and use on the internet. To try them out, the easiest place to go is http://www.compileonline.com Choose the "Learn C++" option down at the bottom, and it will take you to where you need to go.

Here is an example to try. The output should be the words "**Try This**".

```
#include <iostream>

using namespace std;

int main ()
{
        court << "Use This One!";

        return 0;
}
```

Now you can choose to type these codes into the compiler directly, or you can write several, and save them to your computer, and access them whenever, so that you don't have to retype them every time you want to mess with them. You can use several different types of text editors. However, some of them are device type specific. This means they only work on the type of device that you create them on.

The text editors that you can use are OS edit command, Brief, EMACS, epsilon, Windows Notepad, vlm or vl. However, only vlm and vl are multi platform usable. Make sure to save the files with the extension .c or .cpp.

You should start in a text editor to get the rough draft going on your program before you even think of moving to a compiler. This is because once you get to a compiler, it is a lot easier to mess up on your program, and not catch it. However, if you have it laid out in a nice, clean-cut fashion in a text editor, then you should have no problems with getting things going in the compiler.

C++ Compilers

There are many different compilers out there, and a lot of them are pretty expensive. Those compilers are for the elite programmers who have mastered the lower level compilers already. Beginners only need a basic compiler, and most of those are free. However, just like with anything that is free, you have to be careful of what you are getting. There are more bad cheap compliers than good ones out there so on the pretense of being free, I would suggest you paying additional functions past the start up page. These additional functions are usually very cheap anyways so you won't have to break the bank to get them.

One of the most popular compilers available is the GNU C/C++ compiler. It is used most commonly in UNIX and Linux installations. To see if you already have the compiler, pull up the command line in your UNIX/Linux application and type in the following

```
$ g++ -v
```

If the compiler is installed, then you should see this message on the screen:

Using built-in specs.

Target: i386-redhat-linux

Configured with: ../configure –prefix=/usr ......

Thread model: posix

gcc version 4.1.2 20080704 (Red Hat 4.1.2-46)

If this message does not come up on your screen, the compiler either isn't on the computer or you installed it incorrectly and you will need to go through and get it properly installed.

In this book, we will go over how to install using the Windows platform. If you have a different platform, then you should go to http://gcc.gnu.org/install/ and read the instructions on how to download it onto your platform.

To install this compiler on your Windows computer, you will need to first install MinGW. This is the software that makes the compiler compatible with your computer, and it is very important that you have this software, otherwise you will not even be able to download the compiler at all.

To install this software, you can go to the homepage of the software at www.mingw.org and allow it to direct you to where you need to go. Once you install that you should install gcc core, gcc-g++, MinGW runtime and blnutlls, at the bare minimum, but you can install more if you would like. Once you are done with the install, you can run all of the GNU tools from the Command line on Windows.

Now that you have everything set up to where you can run it, you can start learning more about how to run the programs themselves.

Basic Syntax

C++ can be defined as not only the program, but objects that collectively communicate by invoking other methods. When you are working with C++ you should know what four things mean above all else.

Class- This is a template or a blueprint that states the object and its support type, and describes the behaviors of an object. This means that objects are sorted by their behaviors and their actions /supports into classes that fit the description of the object in question.

Object- Objects have behaviors and states. For example, if you look at a dog, it has states. These states could be classified as color, breed, name, standard of breed (AKC/AKA/APC registries). "Dogs" also show certain behaviors as well. They wag their tails, they bark, they pant, they eat dry kibble, and they go to the bathroom outside in the yard. These things make dogs a *unique object*. These objects are classified into groups know as, you guessed it, classes.

Method- This is another term for behavior. There can be as many or as few as you choose in your classes. This is where all of the data is manipulated, and actions are played out, along with the place that all of the logic is written. Methods are especially important because without them, your program would not know what it is supposed to do with the variable that you give it. It would just sit there like a dud and do nothing.

Instant Variables- These refer to each individual object. Each object is classified with a unique set of these variables that act as a fingerprint for an object. These variables are assigned to the object by using values that occur whenever the object is created.

Now that you know the four main definitions of programming, Let's take a look at a code that you can write that will print out: **"Try This"**. Unlike the example above, this will explain a little more in depth what you are wanting to do, and the reason for each function.

```cpp
#include <iostream>

using namespace std;


// main()  [this is when the program will begin
to execute.]


int main()
{
```

```
        cout << "Try This"; // [Prints Try This]

        return 0;

}
```

This function will allow you to print whatever you want, not just the words "Try This".

Now let's break down the various aspects of the program that is set out above. There are several different aspects of this language that you have to take in consideration. Each aspect is important in getting it to run, and if you do not execute them entirely.

Headers- There are several headers out there for C++, and all of them are necessary or at the very least useful to your programming operations. However, for most functions you will see the header that is above <iostream>. When you use a header be sure to enclose it properly, and put **#include before** it to prompt the program to use that header.

Namespace- Namespaces are a fairly new addition to C++, only coming about in the 2011 update. They do not do much, other than describe which namespace to use. While they are not necessary, they save you a lot of confusion on functions of a program. It simply act as a way to organize your functions more systematically.

Main- Here is where the main function begins. Using the line **// main()** instructs the program to start executing the main function of the program, and start the out put process. It is essential that you set up the main function command, otherwise your program will not know what it is supposed to be running, nor will it know when it is supposed to run. This will be seen as a single line comment inside the program and it is going to tell the program that the main function is beginning.

INT main- This is where the function execution officially begins. If you do not include this, the entire process will stop, because you did not introduce the variables, and without the variables, the program is lost.

Cout- This instructs the program to display the message that you want on the screen. If you do not put cout, chances are your program will may or may not fail. The problem is you don't know if you succeed or not so if you want to make sure that everything runs smoothly, be sure to add cout.

Return- This returns the value back to zero, and terminates the function. It instructs the program to end the process, and go back to the beginning.

Now to compile and execute your first official C++ program.

First you must know how to *save* the file. Open your chosen text editor, and enter the code that is seen above. Once you have done that, hit save as, and choose a file location that is easily found. For organization purposes, it is always best to have a separate folder for all of your programs. Save the file as hello.cpp, and once you have saved it, you should open up your command prompt before heading to the directory where the file is saved.

To get the file to open inside your compiler, start by typing 'g++ hello.cpp'. you can then press enter and the code will be opened properly. As long as there aren't any errors, the prompt is going to generate an a.out executable file. To run the program, type out 'o.out' and see the compiler work. The information that you should get on the compiler from this on the computer includes:

$ g++ hello.cpp

$ ./a.out

Try This

Make sure that you are inputting all of the variables the proper way, and remember, these things are case sensitive. If you do not input the functions the right way, you will find that things tend to go awry. The thing with coding is you have to be precise. This detailed oriented personal attributed applies to all programming languages! However, anyone can do it if they are willing to pay attention.

The basic function commands are not the only things that you need to use. There are other things that are important when you are building a prompt as well, as they too instruct the program to do specific things. Some of these things are blocks and semicolons.

You probably think a pause in a sentence when you think semicolon, however, they are complete stops in C++ programs. The semicolon indicates the termination of a statement. This means that each individual statement must be indicated by the use of a semicolon. The following are three different statements.

x=y;

y=y+1;

add(x,y);

Each one of those statements were separated by not only a line break, but also a semicolon. You could also do it this way.

x=y; y=y+1; add(x,y);

Each one of those will be recognized as separate statements simply because of the semicolon. It is kind of mind blowing how something so simple can have so much of an impact.

In this coding language, a block is going to be a set of statements that you enclose with brackets. These statements are logical entities that the program puts on the screen due to the main command prompt. For example

```
{
        cout << "I like Pizza">>; //prints I like Pizza

        return 0
}
```

The end of a line is not a terminator, as was indicated above. The semicolon is the only thing that terminates the statement.

Identifiers

Now let us move on to the identifiers in the program. These identifiers are used to identify multiple things, such as classes, modules, functions and variables within a block. An identifier is going to be a group of letters and numbers that you are able to name your program or your files and they must start with a letter, but can have any letter or number you want afterwards. There are no punctuation characters other than what you might see in a sentence that are allowed as identifiers. You will not see characters such as @,&,% or $, and the programming is case sensitive. That means YokoOno is different than Yokoono, yokoOno, and yokoono. Make sure that you are capitalizing only the letters that you should be capitalizing in your programs.

Though pretty much anything can be an identifier, there are some things that are reserved for keywords in C++, and can't be used as identifiers. These words are as follows.

asm		
Break	Bool	Auto
Char	Catch	Case
Const cast	Const	Class
Delete	Default	Continue
Dynamic cast	Double	Do
Explicit	Enum	Else
False	Extern	Export
Friend	For	Float
Inline	If	Goto
Mutable	Long	Int
Protected	Private	Namespace
Reinterpret cast	Register	Public
Signed	Short	Return
Static cast	Static	Sizeof
Template	Switch	Struct
True	Throw	This
Typeid	Typedef	Try
Unsigned	Unlon	Typename

Void	Virtual	Using
While	Wchar t	Volatile

Everything else is fair game when it comes to identifiers. Think of identifiers as usernames and passwords. Mix it up, but make sure that they are functional.

Trigraphs

Trigraphs are going to be sequences of three characters that will represent just one character. You will notice these because they are going to start out with two questions marks at the beginning. Seems a little redundant to use three characters when one will work, but the reason behind this is so you do not confuse the program with the meaning of the character, as many are similar.

Here are some frequently used trigraphs to give you an example of what we mean.

??=	#
??/	\
??'	^
??(	[
??)	]
??!	|
??<	{
??>	}
??-	~

Not all compilers support trigraphs due to their confusing nature, and most people try to stay away from them, however, it has been found that when you memorize trigraphs, you are less likely to mess up by hitting the wrong symbol in your function.

Whitespace

Moving on to whitespace. This is the empty lines in a program. Sometimes they contain comments, and these are known as blank lines. The compilers completely ignore them. Whitespace describes blanks, new lines, tabs, characters and comments. It is merely used to make your program look more organized and readable.

There should be at least one line of whitespace between the variable/identifier and the statement.

QUIZ

You thought that you could just waltz through this book without being tested on if you were paying attention? No cheating either! Just because you can peek at the answers does not mean that you should. You should take it just like a normal quiz to truly test your knowledge so you can figure out if you need to go back and re-read over some things. This is a short quiz, so you will be okay.

1.   What is whitespace?

2. Fill in the blanks ____ <<x=y+1_>>

3. What are trigraphs?

4. Who Invented the C with Classes language?

5. What is the header used in most functions?

Answers

1. The blank spaces or comments that the compiler ignores

2. Cout <<x=y+1;>>

3. A sequence of three characters that represent a single character

4. Bjarne Strousup

5. <iostream>

Congratulations, if you got all five right, then you can move on to the next section! However, if you got more than one wrong, then you should probably go back and reread the section. If you're ready then onwards to Chapter 3.

Chapter 3: Diving more into Program Comments, Data Types, Lines, and Characters

Now that we have covered the bare basics of C++ it is time to get into some more in depth subjects that surround the program. While these are more in depth, they are still a paramount concepts all beginners need to learn.

Program Comments

So, there are going to be times when you will want to write some comments inside of your code. These are important because they allow you to leave a little message inside the code so that others who are reading through it later on will be able to get a good look at exactly how your code is ran and also provide "referral" to what you're trying to accomplish in your code. Furthermore, leaving notes within the lines of your code is a good way to notify yourself where a code might have gone wrong. By putting comments inside your codes, you are more likely to know where you succeed or where you went wrong.

These comments can be as simple or as complex as you would like. Some people will just place in one or two words if that is all that is needed to help out the other users, but there are other times when you are going to need to combine a few more lines into the mix to ensure that it is all going to work out and that the other person understands what is going on inside of the code.

In this language, you will just need to use the // symbol in order to show that you are writing out a comment. You can make it as long as you would like, just make sure that when the comment is done, you skip to the next line so that the program knows that it is supposed to start reading through it again.

The program is going to stop reading after the // and it is not going to affect the way that the program works. Other programmers who look at the code will see the comments that you write, but when the program is executed, these comments are going to be skipped. You can add in as many as you would like to your program, but do try to keep them a bit limited because it can start to clog up the code and make it hard to read and understand.

Program comments are basically the statements that are inside the code. The statements, or comments, are going to be there to help others who use your code understand what the purpose of each function is. All program languages allow for some type of comments, but they do not allow all of the kinds of comments that are out there. The most common to use is a single line comment. This is what all program languages allow for. These comments are simple explanatory lines that tell the next reader what the purpose is in a simple sentence.

There are also multiple line comments. This is one that very few program languages allow for. C++ is one of those few languages. Sometimes you have a more complex explanation, and it needs to span over more than one line. This is possible to do in C++.

When you are using a single line comment, you will see that it is written out in the code with // and can go all the way to the end of your line. An example of this is:

```
{

        cout << "that's great" >>;  //prints that's great

        return 0

}
```

will have the final output of "that's great" and nothing else. The comment is ignored by the compiler so that you can let other programmers in on what the code is for, or what you need done to the code.

However if you are trying to get some help on a code, you should use a multi line comment so that you can easily get the best out of your complicated code. Multi line comments are surrounded by these symbols /*-*/. Typed out like that it almost looks like an emoji. For example

/* I need help making the puppet dance*/ is a comment. However, that is still a single line comment still. A better example would be

/* I need help making the puppet dance

*All he does at this point is sway from side to side */

That would be a multi line comment. As you can see, when you start a new line you should put the asterisk at the beginning to indicate to the program that you are still writing a comment and that the next line is indeed whitespace. When compiled it will ignore the comments and only show what you want it to show.

While you can mix the comment styles, it is best to keep them separated for now, until you get the hang of everything.

Data Types

You have to use different variables when you are writing a program using any language. These are nothing more than just reserved memory values that store locations in some space in the memory of the compiler. The above list of reserved keywords are useful here as well. While there are a lot of keywords, there are seven basic keywords that define data types.

Type	Keyword
Wide character	Wchar_t
Valueless	Void
Double floating point	Double
Floating point	Float
Integer	Int
Character	Char
Boolean	bool

Most of the data types that you can use can be modified using one of these following modifiers to help:

Long,

Short

Unsigned

Signed

Variable Types Cont...

When you are using variables inside of a coding language, you are providing some storage space that makes it easier to for the program to manipulate. All of the variables that you use will be attached to a different type and these types are going to determine the layout and the size of the memory of the variable. It is also going to set a range of values that you are able to store on this memory space.

Naming the variable is going to be similar to naming the identifier. You will only be able to name it with a letter or an underscore and the letters are going to be case sensitive. But after that, you are able to use any type of digit, letter, and character that you would like.

Again, the basic variables that you will be able to use here in more detail include:

•   Wchart_t: this is the wide character type.

•   Void: this is going to represent the absence of a type

•   Double: this is a floating value that will have double precision.

•   Float: this is a floating point that is going to have single precision.

•   Int: this is an integer

•   Char: this is often going to be just one byte and is a type of integer.

•   Bool: this is going to work with values that are either true or false.

You can also define other types of variables. These variables are things line pointer, array, reference, enumeration, data structures, and classes.

Creating a new line

Now that you know the data types and modifiers, and all about making a comment in your program, it is time to learn about how to create a new line. This is a problem that a lot of new programmers run into. They have their program all nice and laid out in the input, but the output is still really mashed together and really unkempt. This is because they did not properly create a new line. Remember that whitespace is ignored, so you cannot just skip a line, and expect to have a line skipped in your program. You have to indicate to the compiler that you want to start a new line. This is really important, as when you play out your program, you want it to run smoothly. You do not want to see something like this.

Try This Today I ate Pizza and I did math. 6= (7-1) that what I learned today.

You would probably rather see this.

Try This

today I ate pizza and I did math

6=(7-1)

that is what I learned today

To make the distinction, you have to have the right function, as that is what programming relies on, having the correct function.

To create a line break, you have to use the function endl; this will indicate that you want a line break, and you do not even have to add whitespace if you do not want to, though it is recommended because it makes your program easier to read for a human.

For example, this:

```
{
        cout << Try This;>> endl;

        <<Today I ate Pizza and did Math;>>
endl;

        <<6=(7-1);>> endl;

        << That is what I learned today;>> endl;

        return 0
}
```

Looks way better than this:

```
{
        cout << Try This;>> endl; << Today I
ate Pizza and did Math;>> endl; <<6=(7-1);>>
endl; << That is what I learned today;>> endl;

        return 0
}
```

Can you see how confusing that would get for someone reading the code? You want your code file to be easy to read, so that if someone else has to fix something, they can easily find where the mistake has been made. If everything is all jumbled together, then they would not be able to find anything very easily, now would they?

You can also indicate line breaks by using /n This is the same thing as endl; but is a lot faster to type. You can use whichever method you want but choose one and stick with it.

The importance of the basics of C++

I know what you are thinking, why must you know all these nonsense tidbits of information when you are just beginning, and the reason is, if you don't learn them now, you won't think that you will need them in the future, and then when you are reading a program that someone else wrote, you will be wondering what all of those extra characters mean, and why there is so much whitespace. Creating a habit of these simple yet somewhat tedious tasks is paramount if mastering more complicated programming methods. Just like mastering any sort of language, you have to master the basics to master the expert level concepts.

Variable definitions

A variable definitions instructs the compiler how much and where to store and create the variable. It specifies the data type and lists one or more of the variables of the type. For example

type variable_list;

You have to have a valid data type that is listed above. They may contain one or more identifier names as long as they are separated by commas, such as

int ---- j,k,l;

char----c,ch;

float---- f, salary;

double--- d;

Each of these abbreviations instructs the compiler to create variables of that type with those names. Variables can be assigned with an initial value, by indicating such with an equal sign. For example

```
#include <iostream>

using namespace std;

int. main ()

int j=10;

int k=5;

int l=j+k

{

        cout <<l>> endl;

        return o

}
```

You should get the answer 15

You can also declare and define the variables in your program, but that is some higher level stuff, so if you would like to look into it you can google search a tutorial on that.

QUIZ

Here is the set up. You should have one phrase, a math problem, and then the answer to the math problem using said integers. You can make up all of the variables yourself, whatever you want them to be.

```
#using <header>

using namespace std;


int main ()

int _=_
```

```
int _=_

int _=_+_

{
        cout < "";> /n

        < "";> /n

        cout < "int_";> /n

        return 0
}
```

Simply enter your digits in and make sure your numbers add up. After you've done so, rerun the code without relying on copying and pasting the code without the intergers. This way, you'll have a basic understanding of variables and playing with the basic integers operations within C++.

Chapter 4: Arrays, Loops, and Conditions

Believe it or not, you've learned so much already. The basics are really not that hard and now it's just about learning about a few more things and putting concept after concept together to make sure you're becoming a better C++ programmer. Let's keep going.

Arrays

Arrays are a data structure in C++ that will be able to store elements that are basically the same type and also a fixed size. Basically a collection of same type variables. Instead of using the individual variables, you would declare one array of variables such as numbers. To do this you use the numbers 0 to 99 and access each one by an index of the array.

Arrays are going to be memory locations that are continuous. The lowest is always the first element and then the highest element is going to be the last.

Initializing arrays

You can initialize arrays one by one or using a single statement. Example

double balance [5]= {1000.0, 2.0, 3.4, 17.0, 50.0};

The numbers that are found between the bracket can't end up higher than the amount of elements that you are using. This means that you cannot have six sets of numbers when your array title only specified five. However, if you do not specify the size, then an array of just the right size is created. You would type it as follows double balance [] {1000.0, 2.0, 3.4, 17.0, 50.0};

This creates the exact same array as the previous example, only you did not specify the array size so it was created for you. Pretty nifty.

Now that you know how to write an array, it is time to move on to putting it into the actual program. This program is a bit more advanced than the ones before, and has a few more elements. You can look up these elements on www.compileonline.com. You will be directed to a lot of tutorials and there is even a PDF file for you to download.

Here is the formula for your program to assign an array.

#include <iostream>

```cpp
using namespace std;

#include <iomanip>
using std::setw;

int main ()
{
    int n[ 10 ]; //n is an array of ten integers
    // initialize elements of array n to 0
    for ( int i=0; I <10; i++)
    {
        n[i] =i+100; // set ekement at location I to i+ 100
    }
    cout << element << setw(13) << value<< endl:
    //output each array element's value
    for (int j=0; j<10; j++)
    {
        cout << setw(7)<< j << setw(13) <<n[j] << endl;
    }
```

```
        return 0

}
```

This program was able to use the setw() function in order to format the output that you see.

Loop Types

The loop types are used any time that you would like to take one type of code and execute it over and over. These statements are going to be done one right after the other. The loop statement will make it easier to execute these statements as many times as you would like.

There are four types of loops. These loops handle different requirements.

While loop

The While loop is going to continue repeating the loop as long as a certain condition is met. It is going to test out this condition each time it restarts the loop cycle and will do this until the condition is no longer true.

Written like this

while (condition)

{

        statement(s);

}

For Loop

This loop executes a statement sequence over and over again while abbreviating the code that manages the loop variables.

Written like this

```
for ( init; condition; increment)
{
        statement(s);
}
```

Do.. while loop

The Do...while loop is going to be similar to the while statement, but it is going to test the condition when you reach the end of your statement, rather than the beginning.

Written like this

```
do

    {

            statement(s);

}while (condition);
```

Nested loops

The nested loop is going to have a loop that works inside of another loop, to create a continuous loop of loops. This one can get confusing after awhile.

Written like this

```
while (condition)

{

        while (condition)

        {

                statement(s)
```

```
        }

        statement(s) // you can put more
statements

}
```

Why is this important

Eventually you are going to want to branch out. I would highly recommend to further enhance your C++knowledge of the basics to ensure mastery and better understanding of more difficult tasks.

Though these may seem like they are too advanced for some or too easy for others, it's always good to do other practices and tutorials to enrich your programming skills. You can find tutorials at www.compileonline.com. It cannot be stressed enough how much of an essential tool this is. You have to check it out for yourself, and find out just how useful it really is. There are tutorials for other languages as well, not just C++ dabble around and see what you like.

Chapter 5: Working with Operators in C++

With any of the coding languages that you plan to use, it is important that you learn how to use the operators. These are going to help you to tell the program what you would like to do and can make dealing with your own codes so much easier. There are four main types of operators that you are able to use inside your program and they will each tell the program how to behave in a different way. Some of the operators that you will be able to use with the C++ language include:

•   Logical operators

•   Arithmetic operators

•   Assignment operators

•   Relational operators

Let's take a look at how some of these work and how you can bring them out to work well when writing code in the C++ language.

Logical operators

The first type of operator that we are going to use in this guidebook are the logical operators. These are going to help you to compare some of the parts that you are putting into the system. Some of the logical operators that you can work with include:

• (||): this is known as the logical OR. With this one, the condition is going to be true if one of your operands is not zero.

• (&&): this one is known as the logical AND. If you have two operands and they are not zero, your condition is true.

• (!): this is the logical NOT. You will be able to use this to reverse the status of your operand. So if the condition ends up being false, this sign will make it true.

Arithmetic operators

Another of the operators that you are able to use is the arithmetic operators. These are pretty much the same as using math in school. You are going to tell the program to add, subtract, and do other equations with the information that you are providing. Some of the arithmetic operators that you are able to use include:

• 	(+): this is the addition operator that will add together two operands of your choices.

• 	(-): this is the subtraction operator. It is going to take the right hand operand and subtract it from the left hand operand.

• 	(*): this is the operator that makes it possible to do multiplication in the C++ language.

• 	(/): this operator helps you to do division in C++.

• 	(++): this is the increment operator. It is going to increase the value of your operand by one.

• (--): this is the decrement operator. It is going to decrease the operand value by just one.

Assignment operators

The assignment operators will make it easier for you to assign a name to your variable and can help with searching for, saving, and so on with the different parts of the code that you are writing. Some of the assignment operators that you may use inside of C++ include:

• (=): this operator is the simple assignment operator. It is going to assign the value of the operand on the right hand to the one that is on the left.

• (+): this one is called the Add AND operator. It is going to add together the values from both operands and then assigns the sum of these over to the operand on the left side.

• (*=): this is the Multiply AND operator. It is going to multiply both of the operands and then gives the results over to the operand on the left side.

•   (-=): this is the one that will subtract the value of your operand on the right side from the one on the left and then gives this difference to the left operand.

•   (/=): this is the divide and operator. It is going to divide the value that is on the left side from the one on the right side and then assigns this amount to the left side.

There are a few other assignment operators that are available, but they are more advanced so we will just stick with some of these basic ones to help keep things in order!

Relational Operators

Relational operators can be really helpful when you are working inside of the C++ language. Some of the ones that you can use include:

•   (==): this is the operator that is going to check the equality of your two operands. If they are equal, the conditions will be true.

•   (>): this operator is going to check the value of your operands. If the operand on the left side is higher than the one on the right, the condition will be true.

- (<): this operator is basically the opposite of the one above. If you find that the value of your operand on the left side is greater than the one on the right side, the condition will be true.

- (!=): this one is going to check the equality of your two operands and if the values are unequal, your condition is true.

- (<=): this operator is going to check whether the operand on the left side is less than or equal to the operand on the right side. If it meets this criteria, the condition is true.

- (>=): this one is going to check if the value of the operand on the left side is greater or equal to the one on the right side. If it is true, the condition is true.

Chapter 6: Helping C++ to Make Decisions

There are times when you will need the program to make decisions for you. You are able to set it up to act in a certain way based on the information that the user puts into the computer and what you decide needs to be met for the conditions to be true. The decision making is a bit more advanced inside of this system, but you will find that is pretty easy to learn and will open up a lot of ideas that you are able to work with in the C++ system. Let's take a look at some of the things that you are able to do to help the system to make decisions on its own.

Switch Statements

The first decision that we are going to work with inside of this system are the switch statements. These statements are nice because they are going to allow you to check the equality of your variable against a set of values, or cases. The variable that you are trying to check is going to be compared with each of the cases. A good example of the syntax that you are able to use for this include:

```
Switch(expression){
        case constant-expression:
        statement(s);
        break; //optional
        case constant-expression:
        statement(s);
        break; //optional
```

//you can add in as many of these case statements as you would like

```
Default: //Optional
statement(s);
}
```

When you are working inside of these statements, there are a few rules that you should keep in mind. First, the expression of the switch statement should be the integral or enumerated class type. In addition, it can also belong to a class that has a conversion function. With C++, there isn't going to be a limit to the amount of case statements that you add into the syntax so you can make them as long or short as you would like. Just remember that you need to have a colon and a value in each of them.

Once the variable finds a value that it is equal to, it is going to keep running until it finds a break statement. The system finds the break statement, the switch is going to stop. Then the control flow will be passed on. You don't need to put in a break statement to the cases. If you end up not having one of these, the control flow will just keep being passed on.

The if statements

One of the most basic things that you are able to do in your programs is create an if statement. These are going to be based on a true and false idea inside the system. If the system says that the input is true with the condition that you set out, then the program is going to run whatever you ask it to. For example, you set it up to have the system as what the answer to 2 + 2 is. If the user puts in the answer as 4, you could have a message come up that says "That is Correct! Good Job!"

Any time that the user puts in an input that ends up being true based on the conditions that you are setting out, you are going to get the statement to show up that you picked out. On the other hand, what is going to happen if your person puts in the wrong answer. If they put the answer as 5 to the question above, it is not going to be right and the system is going to see that the answer is false.

Since the if statement is pretty basic, you are going to find that it is not going to be prepared if the person puts in the wrong answer. At this stage, if they put in any number other than 4 for the example above, the screen is just going to go blank and nothing is going to happen. The next type of statement will go more in depth and show you how to get answers based on what the person puts into the system.

The if else statement

Now as we discussed a bit above, there are some limitations that can come up when you are using the if statement. If the person puts in the wrong answer, the screen is just going to go blank and this can be a pain with the system. Plus, there are times when the user will need to put in a variety of answers, such as when they will put in their age and you want to separate those out. Their age is not necessarily wrong, but if you just want people who are older than 21, you want to make sure that an answer comes up correctly along the way.

A good syntax to use in order to work with the if else statements include:

if(boolean_expresion)

{

        //statement(s) will execute if the boolean expression is true

}

Else

{

```
    // statement(s) will execute if the
boolean expression is false

}
```

You are able to add in as many of these into your statement as you would like. So if you would like to have a program that set apart people in five different age groups, you could set that up based on more of the "else" in your syntax. This makes it easier to add in some other choices.

So let's keep it simple. Let's say that you have 2 +2 on the system. If the person guesses that 4 is the answer, you can set that up in the first part to be the true statement and then the message "That's Right! Good Job!" will come up on the screen. But if the user puts in the answer 5 (or any other answer than 4), you can have a message like "Sorry, that is not the right answer" come up on the screen.

This gives you a lot of freedom when it comes to taking care of what you want to do inside of your code. You are going to be able to add in some different things to the process and you

can really expand the code that you are
working on.

Another thing that you can keep in mind when
working on these, is that you are able to add
some if statements and some if else statements
inside of each other. This can get a bit complex
as a beginner, but with some practice, you will
find that it is going to add a lot of power to the
whole process and can make it easier to do
some of the things that you want within this
coding language.

Working with the if statements and the if else
statements can make your coding experience so
much better. It allows the system to make
decisions based on what the user is putting into
the system rather than having to be there and
do it themselves. Make sure to try out a few of
these different types of statements and see how
they are going to work within your code and
with what you want to do.

Chapter 6: Constants and the various types of Literals

This language is complex, and even though what you have learned above is enough to run some simple functions, there are so many more parts to this language that it would be a crime to not put more in depth knowledge in here to help you transition to the next step.

If you want to be successful with this language, be prepared to spend long hours working hard on it. While it is a good language for beginners as it has multiple levels of difficulties, it is also something that you have to work hard at to make it to the next level. The added effects are more difficult the more you try to learn.

Programming itself is a long and difficult process, but it is definitely worth it, as there are so many professions that you can go into that require the knowledge of C++. From game designing, to working with robots and more. If it involves technology, chances are it involves C++.

So here are some more steps that you can learn, and some more important functions that you need to know to begin to master this language.

Constants and Literals

Constants and literals are an imperative part of learning C++. They refer to data types and variables in those data types. They are constant, and cannot be changed.

They act just like any other variable, other than the fact that they are stagnant and you cannot change them. The integers that you use are known as literal integers. They can have a suffix such as U or L, and they stand for unassigned, and long. These variables are used as uppercase and lowercase and can help your processes along well.

To understand the integer literals, look at some of these examples:

032uu	//illegal: can't repeat your suffix
078 octal digit	//illegal: 8 isn't considered an
Ox_Fell	//this one is legal
215	//this one is legal
212	//this one is legal
85	//this one is a decimal
30ul	//this one is an unsigned long
30l	//this one is long
30u	//this one is an unsigned int.
30	//tis one is an int.
Ox4b	//this one is a hexadecimal
0213	//this one is an octal

Floating Point Literals

These are parts of the code that will contain an integer, a decimal point, a fractional part, and an exponent part. These can be shown either through the exponential form or the decimal form.

When you choose to use the decimal point to represent these literals, you need to make sure that you are adding in at least the decimal, although adding in the exponent is good as well. When you are representing through the exponential form, you should include either the fractional part, the integer part, or both of them. The signed exponent that you are using should also be started with either E or e.

Some of the floating point literals that you are able to use in your code writing include:

.e55   //these are illegal because they are missing the fraction or the integer

210f: //these are illegal because they don't have the exponent or the decimal

510E //these are illegal because they have an incomplete exponent

314159E-5L //these are legal

3.15159   //these are legal

Boolean Literals

The next type of literal that we can discuss are the Boolean literals. There are two types that you will be able to use inside of your C++ code. Basically the Boolean values are going to be shown as either true or false. If the conditions that you set out are true, the Boolean expression is going to come out as true. On the other hand, if the conditions that you set out are not met, you are going to end up with a condition that is false. All of the answers when they are Boolean will come out either true or false.

Character Literals

When you see a character literal in your code, you will notice that they are closed off with single quotes. These can be simple and use something like 'x' to tell the command or they can be much longer in length as well. These are basic things that you are able to add into your code and can make things much easier to handle.

String Literals

Another type of literal that you are able to work with are the string literals. These are the ones that will be closed off using a double quote. The string is going to contain characters that are like the character literals, including options like universal, escape sequence, and plain characters. You can use the string literal in many ways including to break up one of your lines into two, and separating out things to make it easier to read. Some of the examples of the strings that you can use include:

hello, Mother"

"hello, \

Mother"

"hello, " "M" "other"

Learning how to use some of these different parts inside of the C++ programming language will make a big difference in how well you are able to use this computer language. Have some fun and experiment with using them a bit and you will find that it is easier than ever to get the results that you want!

Conclusion

Thank you again for purchasing this book. I hope that it proved to be informational, but enjoyable. Keep this book as a guide not only for knowledge, but inspiration as well. C++ seems like an intimidating language but the more you practice it in regularity, by days, months, and years, you will achieve complete mastery of this programming language like with anything else in life. I ask you not to fret and be anxious and a problem arise, because there will be many times in which this will happen. There are numerous resources out there for you just waiting to be read of discovered and it is in your best interest to do your due diligence in learning, improving, and enhancing your C++ programming skills to the next level.

Bonus: Brief Hacking History and Overview

Many people have heard the name C++ but really think nothing of it. If you are not very technologically versed then you may think that it is about having a mediocre letter grade, but that is not the case.

Believe it or not, C++ is a hacking language, and while it is not the only one out there, it is one of the more important ones because it is versatile and also easy to use. To learn the most about C++, you have to know more about the reason it came about and that would be hacking.

Hacking

Hacking is not a new concept. For as long as there has been any type of technologies around, there have been people figuring out ways to hack them. Hacking is the manipulations and/or interruptions of any technological stream of data that is being sent from one place to another. This is done with scripts. While you can get pre-packaged scripts online, many people prefer the old fashioned way of writing their own scripts, as is gives them more flexibility to do what the want with the information. Scripts that come already set up into packages have limited mobility and are pretty visible. The goal of a hacker who truly wants to hack is to remain discreet. If you are caught, unless you have permission to be doing what you are doing, you can get in a heap of trouble.

History of Hacking

Hacking began officially in the 1970s when teenagers were banned from using the phone lines because they were trying to make free calls, and figured out how to do so. Phone hacking was the biggest thing, and continued for over a hundred years. Making calls used to be expensive, especially when the phone lines were new, so of course people were trying to find ways to save money, and usually it caught up with them. Such was the case for a man named John Draper. He was arrested for figuring out how to make long distance calls simply by blowing a note into the receiver that prompted it to make a long distance call without an operator. You could then input the number and talk as long as you wish. Genius, but illegal.

He started a revolution though. A group of young teens banded together to create a phone line that hacked the system to help people make free calls. Once this spread like wild fire, Steve Jobs decided to come up with a product that he could market that hacked the phone lines and helped people make free calls by themselves.

Big time computer hacking didn't actually start until the 1980s. However, once it began, it spread like wildfire, and there were a lot of people who thought that it would be a great idea to see what all they could do, and how they could manipulate these computers.

Types of Hacking

There are several different types of hacking out there. And while the media portrays all hackers as bad, they are not. It is not black and white either. While those are the two most popular groups when talking about hacking, there are so many categories in between, that it would not be beneficial to only talk about the two that are most known.

The two main categories that all the sub categories fall between however, are ethical and unethical hacking.

Ethical hacking is hacking that is used only for good purposes. There are a lot of people who have full permissions to hack into a system, and to find all of the bugs of the software or hardware.

Ethical hackers are the ones that are responsible for all of the bug fixes in your phone, apps, tablets, or computers. These people are hired by a company to figure out what is wrong with their systems, and find the best way to fix it. These hackers are an essential part of the hacking community.

If it were not for hackers we would not have the world wide web, urls or HTML. Hacking is an important part if done within the boundaries of ethical hacking.

Unethical hacking, however, is not within the realms of hacking that is legal with current laws. It is hacking for a malicious purpose. People who hack bank mainframes and steal people's credit card and account information and use it to drain accounts are known as unethical hacking.

Unethical hacking is the bane of true hackers existence. These people are the ones that give the good guys a bad name.

Now to go on to the terms for all different types of hackers.

- White Hat Hackers: These are the completely ethical hackers. Every thing that they do is done for good. They go thru a system, and comb it down for any bugs, and build super strong firewalls so that the systems are safe. They create anti-malware software.

- Black Hat Hacking: This is the type of hacking that you have to stay away from. With great power comes great responsibility. The great responsibility to not become prey to the temptation that is black hat hacking. This type of hacking can get you in a lot of trouble, and are immoral. Hacking government files or even other people's privacy can be tempting but will lead to heavy disciplinary actions.

- Grey Hat Hacking: These are the hackers that sometimes do bad things for good reasons. Such as Anonymous. They may hack the firewall of an sensitive information file, but they do so to expose the corruption that is going on behind the firewall. These hackers are often treated like criminals, but in reality, they can be regarded as heroes depending on your perspective.

- Red Hats: These are the bounty hunters of the hacking world. They use their hacking skills to find illegal hackers, such as black hat hackers, or grey hats that are doing bad things that they should not be doing. They then turn them over to the feds, so that the illegal hackers are arrested. There are several other terms for these hackers, but they are not very appropriate, so we shall leave them out.

- Blue Hat Hackers: These are the blue collar workers of the hacking world. They sit in a cubicle and hack away all day to find bugs for Microsoft or other major companies. They clock into a nine to five job that just happens to involve hacking.

These are the main classifications of hackers. There are also elite hackers that spend their entire life becoming the best hackers that the world has seen, and green hat hackers who don't really care about hacking, they just do it for fun. Hacking can be a very useful tool, and even become a profession if you go about it the right way.

Now it is important to note that all of these hackers are going to work in a different way, but they are going to use the same kinds of codes in order to get the information that they want from other computers. A black hat hacker is going to concentrate on getting into the system and getting the information that they need to see success while the white hat hackers are going to work to keep these hackers off the system. While they are working in different ways, they are going to use the same tools and see who will come out on top in the end.

With that said, you need to be careful about what you are doing with your hacking abilities. If you are using them to get onto a system or a network that you aren't allowed to be on, then you could get into a lot of trouble. While some people find these vulnerabilities and tell the company all about them right away, it is still a legal issue if you are on the system when you shouldn't be. The company you mess with could press charges so it is always best to just work within your own network and keep that safe rather than trying to get onto a network you don't belong.

On the other hand, if you are someone who loves to work in the computer world and you want to be able to do this all the time, it may be a good idea to work as a white hat hacker. There are many companies that hold onto private and personal information for their customers, whether it is hospital information, credit card information, or something else. They are always on the lookout for a black hat hacker who may try to get into the system and take this information and a good white hat hacker can always find the work that they need helping these companies out.

Hacking University: Junior Edition. Learn Python Computer Programming from Scratch

Become a Python Zero to Hero. The Ultimate Beginners Guide in Mastering the Python Language

BY: ISAAC D. CODY

HACKING UNIVERSITY

UNIVERSITY

JUNIOR EDITION

Learn Python Computer Programming from Scratch

Become a Python Zero to Hero. The Ultimate Beginners
Guide in Mastering the Python Language

ISAAC D. CODY

Table of Contents

responsibility or blame be held against the publisher for any reparation, damages, or monetary loss due to the information herein, either directly or indirectly.

Respective authors own all copyrights not held by the publisher.

The information herein is offered for informational purposes solely, and is universal as so. The presentation of the information is without contract or any type of guarantee assurance.

The trademarks that are used are without any consent, and the publication of the trademark is without permission or backing by the trademark owner. All trademarks and brands within this book are for clarifying purposes only and are the owned by the owners themselves, not affiliated with this document.

Disclaimer

Introduction

Thank you for downloading the book *"Hacking University: Junior Edition. Learn Python Computer Programming from Scratch. Become a Python Zero to Hero. The Ultimate Beginners Guide in Mastering the Python Language."*

Python is a powerful and highly recommended language for beginners for a variety of reasons. This book serves as a beginners guide for those that have never written programming code before, so even if the thought of programming is daunting this book can explain it in simple terms. We will introduce the process from the very beginning with actual code examples; follow along to learn a valuable computer skill that can potentially land you a job working with the elegant Python language.

Related Software

For enhancing your Python skill, use an IDE. If you have not downloaded it yet, Atom is highly recommended for Python programming. Atom is customizable, in that you can install add-ons at any time to make programming easier. "autocomplete-python" is one such add-on that can guess what you are typing and automatically fill in the rest of the command.

VI and Emacs are two other popular text editors for programmers. Both are considered highly advanced and optimized for writing code, but a bit of a "flame war" exists between fans of both softwares. For the Linux Python programmer, investigate the two text editors and test whether it helps with Python workflow.

After you have finished a particularly useful Python program and wish to distribute it to users, you have to keep in mind that many of them do not have Python installed and will likely not want to install it just to run your program. PyInstaller (http://www.pyinstaller.org/) is a piece of software that builds your Python script and the needed modules into an .exe file that does not need Python to run. It is a handy software should distribute your applications.

Online Resources

For obtaining online help related to Python, you can always check the online documentation (https://www.python.org/doc/). The documentation contains examples and manual pages for every function built-in to Python and its included modules.

For times when programming code just does not work, you can always turn to search engines to resolve your problem. Typing in the error text into Google can turn up other programmers who also had the same problem and posted online. If the problem cannot be fixed by observing other code, websites such as Stack Overflow (http://stackoverflow.com/) are notoriously helpful in resolving code issues. Make an account their and post your problem politely and somebody will probably help you out.

Finally, there are websites that offer tutorials online about how to learn intermediate and advanced Python

programming.
http://www.learnpython.org/ is one
particularly exemplary one, but the
sheer amount comes from the fact that
Python is highly used and well
understood. For any time Python help is
needed, a quick internet search may
solve your curiosities.

The Job Market

As a popular language and because of its widely implemented use, Python jobs are abundant. Large companies and start-ups alike are looking for programmers that understand Python, and because Python is still increasing in use the jobs prospects will continue to increase.

Most companies do not require college education for programming jobs, because they understand that most programmers are self-taught. Obtaining a job in the Python job market is not difficult because of this, but it still requires preparation and dedication on the programmer's part. Younger Python programmers can gain internships at Google, Apple, Intel, and more just by showing a drive to learn. Adult Python programmers can apply for programming jobs by directly contacting companies or replying to job listings. Search online in message boards, job sites, and freelance websites such as UpWork for prospects. Also ask around programming groups and attend job fairs to learn about companies that are hiring Python programmers.

Build a decent résumé and be prepared to prove your knowledge with the language. The interview process for programming jobs often contain "whiteboard" programming tests where you are presented with a situation and asked to use Python to solve the issue. They will not be too terribly difficult, but you certainly need to have a decent grasp on Python to pass.

Overall, finding a Python job is easy because of the current market, but also difficult because you need to know Python intimately. Dedicate yourself to applying for as many positions as possible and eventually a job will appear.

History of Python

Python is a programming language with origins in the late 1980's. Guido van Rossum, the creator, was looking to develop a language as a hobby project to supersede the ABC programming language. Taking cues from the popular C language, Python was created to be a powerful but easy to understand scripting language.

The term "scripting language" refers to the fact that written code is not actually compiled, but rather it is interpreted by an application. Normally this means that scripting languages are not nearly as powerful as actual programming languages. For Python, though, the opposite is true- the language remains one of the most powerful available for web servers and desktop clients. Development of Python continued throughout the 1990's until version 2 was released in 2000. The interpreter behind Python became intricate enough that current versions of Python are almost indistinguishable from lower level programming languages.

Throughout the mid 2000's and even now, Python continues to be developed by Guido van Rossum and a team of dedicated volunteers. The language gained great popularity due to its many benefits, and popular websites such as YouTube, Reddit, and Instagram even use Python for functionality. It seems as though Python will continue to grow for many more years as companies adopt the easy to use but highly useful Python language.

Why Use Python?

When first starting out learning how to program, the huge amount of options, information, and advice can be truly intimidating. Some experts claim that the difficult but time-honored C language is the best start, but other professionals say starting on an easier language such as Java or Python will give the learner a chance to actually absorb key concepts. Python is recommended for this exact reason-programming will not be as foreign and confusing by starting with a straightforward scripting language.

Python is easy to understand, an elegant and clean language, and free of many of the complicated symbols and markings that are used elsewhere. Often accomplishing a task using Python only requires a few lines of neatly formatted code.

Large companies such as Google, Disney, NASA, and Yahoo all use Python for their own programs; having Python knowledge could potentially land a programmer a job working at a high-profile organization. Moreover, because Python is continuously developed today with new features always being added, interest in the language will continuously increase with time. More companies will discover that Python is an exceedingly useful programming language, so learning it now will prepare you for the future.

Benefits of Python

In addition to being easy and fast, Python also has various other benefits. Python is very portable, meaning that Python code can run on a variety of different operating systems. Windows, Mac OSX and Linux distributions are all supported directly, and code written on one platform can be used on all of them.

Power is not compromised by Python's ease-of-use. The interpreter behind the scripting language is able to turn near-natural English commands into low-level processor instructions that put it on par with actual programming languages. Big-name companies choose to use Python because of this, and as websites such as YouTube and Pinterest prove, Python has a wide range of functionality.

Python is clean and retains a focus on readable code. Style and formatting are usually left up to individual programmers, but with Python neatness is absolutely required. For beginner programmers this instills good programming practices, which will dually help with Python and any other languages the novice wishes to learn.

Ease of development and testing also propel Python above other similar languages. Code can be run instantly with the interpreter which allows for rapid prototyping. Being able to quickly test out code means that bugs can be fixed quickly, allowing more time for other development goals.

Conclusively, Python is the perfect language for beginners. Both simple to develop for and learn, Python is also decently powerful. Fantastic for newcomers and those just starting out programming, Python remains the top choice of technology companies everywhere. Learning the language will prove to be useful now and into the future as its popularity continues to grow.

Setting up a Development Environment

Programming languages are typically used on Linux-based operating systems such as Ubuntu and Debian. Python is no exception, but there is another option of developing on Windows. This book will explain how to get both set up. It is important to know though, that we will develop with Python 3, rather than the older (but still extremely popular) Python 2.7.

Most Linux distributions actually come with Python installed by default. Therefore, there are no extra setup procedures to obtaining a working environment. The Python interpreter can be entered by typing "python" into a terminal console. If there are multiple versions installed, though, "python" will start the first one found. Check the version number in the interpreter, and if 2.7 launches you might have to type "python3" into the terminal instead. Press ctlr+c to quit out of the interpreter at any time.

Windows computers usually never have Python preinstalled. To obtain the software, navigate to the Python website and download the most recent version. As of now, Python 3.5.2 is the current version. So long as your version number is Python 3, the code written in this book should also be compatible. Install the software with mostly default settings. Definitely check the "Add Python to the Path", because it simplifies testing programs. After the installer is done the Python interpreter can be started by searching for "python" in the start menu.

The interpreter, or parser, is one of Python's advertised features that allows for individual lines to be written and run. For testing out code the parser is fantastic, but mostly every program we write in this book will be multiline, so we will need an IDE (integrated Development Environment). Windows has a few popular solutions, such as Atom, Pycharm, and Eclipse. These are all 3rd party applications that can be downloaded and installed. IDEs are essentially glorified text editors that offer helpful programming features such as syntax highlighting and command-completion. Although Atom is highly recommended for Windows developers, Python comes with an IDE solution already. IDLE is an interpreter program that can be made multiline by clicking on "file" and then "new file". Whether you choose to use the preinstalled editor or choose to get a full-fledged programming environment through Atom/Eclipse, the Python code will work just the same. You will write your code within one of the multiline programs.

On Linux you also have the option of downloading a Python-compatible IDE application, but most programmers tend to use the preinstalled application "nano". Nano is a built-in, barebones text editor accessible by typing "nano" into a console. The program can actually do some rudimentary syntax highlighting once it knows a Python script is being written, so many developers prefer the basic setup provided. Code is written into nano, then saved by pressing ctrl+x.

Now that there is a development environment set up, you can continue onwards to begin writing your first Python program.

Hello World

Mostly every programmer gets introduced to a new language by writing the "Hello World" program. Hello World is traditionally a simple exercise that involves displaying the titular text on the screen. To do it in Python, we must open up our IDE or text editor and simply type the function.

print ("Hello, World!")

Next, we save the file. In IDLE (and most IDEs such as Atom) one must go through "file" and click "save as". In Nano ctrl+x must be pressed. Name the file with a ".py" extension and save it in an easily accessible directory- your desktop is perfectly fine. For this demonstration we will name the file "test.py".

Running a Python file differs slightly between platforms. Windows must use the command prompt, while Linux must use the terminal. Open up the respective application (ctrl+R and then cmd for Windows, ctrl+T for Linux). These applications are text-based interfaces that can be used to navigate and interact with a computer. The printed line will tell which directory you are currently located in, and you can type "dir" in Windows or "ls" in Linux to display a list of files in that directory. Move to another folder by typing "cd" followed by the directory name. Since we have saved the file to the desktop, on both operating systems we can make it active by typing "cd Desktop". Finally, the Hello World script can be run by typing "python test.py" or "python3 test.py" (on Linux).

If the above programming code was copied exactly, the output "Hello, World!" will be seen. The program will run and then exit back to terminal/prompt. Not entirely glamourous, but a worthy first step into learning Python.

Programming Concepts

In the above program, "print" is referred to as a command or function. Each function has a specific syntax that must be followed. For example, after print there is a set of parenthesis. Values passed within parenthesis are called parameters. Quotations also surround our text, and that is syntax that specifies written text, or a string. The syntax of print must be followed exactly, or else a syntax error will be returned when the program tries to run. As new functions are introduced in this book, careful attention must be placed upon following the syntax rules.

Anything can be put within the quotations of the print function and it will be written to the console. Since Python starts at the beginning of a script and reads lines individually, multiple print functions can be placed one after another like so:

print ("Hello, World!")

print ("This is my 2nd Python Program")

print ("Notice how each print command puts the text on a new line!")

After saving and running the file, all three functions will print their respective parameters. As mentioned previously, the quotations explain that text will be displayed. By forgoing quotations, numbers can be displayed instead.

print ("The answer to everything is:")

print (42)

Python starts at the beginning of the script file and works its way down one line at a time until no more lines are found, in which case the program exits back to prompt or terminal.

Variables

Computers have the ability to "remember" data by storing the values as variables. Variables are RAM locations that are set aside to contain a value. Programming languages must specifically declare variables and assign them by writing code. Being able to manipulate data will prove to be a valuable asset when creating applications.

Creating a variable is known as "declaration". Giving a value is known as "assigning". Python simplifies the process by combining the two concepts into a single statement. Within a program the following line will create a variable:

lucky_number = 7

And then we can use the print function to view the variable we created.

```
print (lucky_number)
```

Because Python starts at the top of a program and works downwards, the above lines need to be in the correct order. If lucky_number is not first created, then print() will return an error for attempting to call a variable that does not yet exist.

An important distinction that can be made is seen when closely viewing the previous print() parameter. The variable lucky_number is not placed within quotations, so Python knows to print the value contained within (7). If we placed quotations around the text, Python would print "lucky_number", which was not our intended result. This situation is referred to as a logic error.

Variable Types

Variables can contain values of multiple types. Our first variable was assigned a numerical value, but Python has methods for handling values of different types as well.

secret_message = "rosebud"

print (secret_message)

As shown above, we can assign a string of text to a variable as well. The process is nearly the same, but notice the quotations around the value that explicitly indicate a string. Here are the most important data types in Python 3:

- Integer – Simple numerical value as a whole number.
    - 1, 0, -7

- Float – Decimal value. "Floating Point Number".
  - 3.0, -7.6, 1.0100001

- String – Letters, words, or entire phrases. Contained within quotation marks.
  - "Hello, world", "no", "12"

- Lists/Tuples/Dictionaries – Multiple related values grouped together as one object. Can be a variety of data types.
  - [1, 4, 4, 0], ["Dog", 2, "yes"]

Obviously, numerical values are declared by simply supplying an integer in the variable declaration. If there is a decimal involved, it will a float. Quotations signify strings, and brackets are for lists.

Variables can also be used in equations, or altered and changed mid-

program. Write the following lines to a
script.

first_num = 2

result = 3 + first_num

print (result)

first_num = 3

result = 3 + first_num

print (result)

You can observe that the value 2 is
assigned to first_num. Then, we create
a new variable "result" that is equal to a
short mathematical expression. 3 and 2
are added and assigned to the result,
which is printed as 5. Then, first_num
is updated to contain a new value.
Result is calculated again and the new
result is printed out. This program

shows how easy it is to use variables within assignments, and how variables can be edited at any time in the program.

More arithmetic operations can be done to numerical variables by specifying an operator in the equation. The following list explains the 5 main operators and the symbol that is used to perform the sequence.

- Addition (+) – Combining numbers

- Subtraction (-) – Taking the difference of numbers

- Multiplication (*) – Repeated addition

- Division (/) – Grouping, or the opposite of multiplication

- Modulus (%) – Dividing and using the remainder as an answer

Both integers and floats can easily perform calculations using the above operators. Note, though, that integers will generally return integer answers (whole numbers) while floats will always return an answer with a decimal point. Python can usually transform an integer into a float when it is needed, but good programming form comes from choosing the correct data type at the appropriate time. For example, see how floats are used in the program below:

first_number = 5.0

second_number = 3.0

result = first_number / second_number

print (result)

And the console will return 1.666666 as an answer. Whereas if integers were used everything past the decimal would be left off for an answer of 1. Assigning the answer to the result variable is not entirely necessary in our small program, and we can rewrite it like so:

first_number = 5.0

second_number = 3.0

print (first_number / second_number)

String variables are not edited mathematically (as in 1 + "two" would not return 3). Instead, the remarks are changed by simply overwriting the words.

name = "Bob"

name = "Bill"

```
print (name)
```

Name will initially be created as the string "Bob", but "Bill" is assigned to it directly after. So when print() is called, the string only contains "Bill". Operators can be used, however, to combine separate strings.

```
my_string = "Hello,"
```

```
my_string2 = "World! "
```

```
print (my_string + my_string2)
```

```
print (my_string2 * 3)
```

The output would be "Hello, World!" for the first print(), and "World! World! World!" for the second print(). The addition operator combines two strings together into one massive string, and the multiplication operator repeats a string the specified number of times.

Input

Although what we have learned so far is interesting, predetermined applications are not very useful for the end user. Python allows us, though, to obtain input from the user to add a layer of interactivity within our scripts. The input() function assigns input to a variable.

favorite_number = input ("What is your favorite number? ")

When a program reaches this line, it will display the text specified and wait for user input. Whatever is input will be assigned to favorite_number, which can be called just as any other variable.

print ("Your favorite number is", favorite_number)

Instead of using an addition operand, we use a comma instead. In print(), commas are used to combine multiple print statements into one (on the same line). We could have used either method, but operators cannot be used for differing data types. Both data types are strings in this case, so it all still works.

The answer that the user gives through input() will always be a string, though. If we were seeking a numerical answer we would have to convert it. Another function, int() can be used to extract numerical data from a string.

favorite_number = int(input ("What is your favorite number? "))

print ("Your favorite number plus 2 is ", favorite_number + 2)

There are a lot of new nuances going on in this program. For example, int() is used to convert the input into an integer. Notice how int() surrounds the entire input() function, which happens because input() must be passed as the entire parameter of int(). Next, the print statement is printing multiple bits of output, and the equation "favorite_number + 2" is evaluated before being printed.

Using int() will always return an integer answer, but float() could have been used to extract a decimal answer instead. The int() function works essentially by transforming the string "3" into the number 3. Definitely remember to include it whenever getting numerical input.

String Formatting

Being able to display strings with print() is useful, but sometimes our programs require us to display variables within them. To actually insert a variable into a string without first editing it or combining multiple variables, we can use a "string formatter". The format() function can be included within a print() statement to do positional formatting of variables.

dog_name = "Rex"

print ("My dog's name is {} and he is a good boy.".format(dog_name))

When you run the above code, it automatically replaced the brackets {} with the supplied variable. The format() is placed directly after the string it will be editing, and before the closing parenthesis. So when the code is run, the console outputs "My dog's name is Rex...". Without using format(), we would have had to use a multi-line complicated print setup. But format()'s greatest use comes from situations with multiple variables.

dog_name = "Rex"

dog_age = 12

print ("My dog's name is {0} and he is {1}. Sit, {0}!".format(dog_name, dog_age))

Here we choose to specify values within the curly brackets. 0 translates to the first supplied parameter, while 1 refers to the second variable. Therefore anywhere in our string we can use {0} to have dog_name be inserted and {1} to have dog_age be inserted. The console text will be "My dog's name is Rex and he is 12. Sit, Rex!"

Example Program 1 – project1.py

```python
user_name = input("What is your name? ")

user_age = int(input("What is your age? "))

user_pets = int(input("How many pets do you have? "))

user_GPA = float(input("what is your GPA? "))

print () #print a blank line

print ("{0} is {1} years old. They have a {3} GPA, probably because they have {2} pets.".format(user_name, user_age, user_pets, user_GPA))
```

This program combines what we have learned so far to obtain input from the user and display it back to them. A new concept, comments are introduced as well. The # symbol is used to denote a comment, or a block of text for human reading. Whenever a # is placed on a line everything after it is ignored by Python. Comments are used primarily to explain things to other programmers that might happen to read your code. In our case, we explain that a blank print() line simply produces a blank line. It is good programming form to use comments throughout your code to explain potentially confusing elements or help remind yourself of what certain blocks of code are doing.

Next, the format() function is used to replace 4 different instances within a print() function. As you might have noticed, counting begins with 0 in Python. 0 always refers to the first element of something, which is why 3 indicates the fourth supplied variable in our format().

Depending upon the medium in which you are reading this publication, some of the above lines may have word-wrapped to multiple lines. This is not how you should be typing it into a text editor though, as the print() line is one single command. Furthermore, copy and pasting from this document may introduce extra characters that Python does not understand. Therefore the correct way to input project 1's code is by typing it out yourself.

Homework program:

- Make a program that obtains information about a user's pet and returns it back.

Decision Structures

Now that the basics of Python 3 are explained, we can begin to offer truly interactive programs by implementing decision structures into our code. Decision structures are pieces of code (called conditional statements) that evaluate an expression and branch the program down differing paths based on the outcome. Observe the following example:

```python
user_input = int(input("What is 4 / 2? "))

if (user_input == 2):

    print ("Correct!")

else:

    print ("Incorrect...")
```

First we obtain input from the user. We test user_input against 2 (the correct answer). If the conditional statement turns out true, then the program will print "Correct!". However, if the user provides the wrong answer Python will return "Incorrect...". There is a lot of new concepts going on here, so we will break it down line by line.

The first line is familiar to us; it obtains input, converting it into an integer and assigning it to the variable user_input. Line 2 introduces a new function- an "if statement". If statements are conditionals that evaluate the expression contained within the parenthesis. Our exact statement checks to see if user_input is 2, and if it is than the immediately following line of code is run. Comparisons use the "==" operator instead of the "=" operator. Double equal signs are checking for equality while single equal signs are only used to assign variables. Lastly, a colon follows the if statement.

Indentations are used extensively in Python to separate off blocks of code. Under the if statement is a tabbed line with a print() function. Because this line is tabbed in, it will not run normally in code. Rather, the line will only run if the conditional if statement is proven true. Because our user input 3 the conditional will evaluate to "False" and the "Correct!" line will not run. Instead the program moves on to the "else statement". Else is a keyword that means "run when the if statement fails". Another indented line follows the conditional, but this time the indented code actually runs because else becomes activated.

If the user had input the correct answer of 2 instead, the if statement would evaluate to true and the console would print "Correct". In that situation, the else statement would not run at all. Focus once again on the indented code and understand that those lines are indented because they are part of the "if" and "else" code blocks. Also realize that only one statement from a decision structure can ever run in a program, so if "else" runs, that means "if" did not run. Likewise a program that has "if" activated will not run the code block under "else". Conditional statements are not limited to single lines of code, as you can see below.

```
user_input = input("What language is this written in? ")

if (user_input == "Python"):

    print ("Correct!")

else:

    print ("Incorrect...")

    print ("This is not written in {}, it uses Python!".format(user_input))
```

Another indented line is within the else code block, and both lines will run if the user does not correctly input "Python". This program does indeed compare strings, so quotations must surround the text.

Conditional Operators

Double equal signs (==) are only one of the many operators that can be used to create a conditional expression. This small list shows other operators in Python.

- \> - Greater than

- \< - Less than

- == - Equal to

- >= - Greater than or equal to

- <= - Less than or equal to

- != - Not equal to

If statements evaluate whether the expression in the parenthesis is true; the above operators allow for some interesting expressions.

```
age =  int(input("How old are you? "))


if (age <= 18):


    print ("Starting early!  Good for you!")
else:


    print ("Ah, a good age to learn.")


print ("Thank you for downloading this book.")
```

A clever use of indentations is used here. If the user's age is 18 or under, it will congratulate them then skip the else statement and finally print out the thank you message. If the user is above 18 it will display the else message and then also thank them. No matter which conditional runs, the user will still receive the thank you message. The indentation makes all the difference about what code lines will actually run within a decision structure, and you must pay close attention to avoid a logic error.

For situations that require more than just two potential outcomes, the keyword "elif" can be used.

```
age =  int(input("How old are you? "))

if (age <= 18 and age > 0):

    print ("Starting early!  Good for you!")

elif (age >= 80):

    print ("Never too late to learn!")

elif (age > 18 and age < 80):
```

```python
    print ("Ah, a good age to learn.")


else:


    print ("That seems like an invalid
age.")
    quit()


print ("Thank you for downloading this
book.")
```

Elif is a keyword that can be used to split the decision making process into multiple branching paths. Between if and else statements, any number of elif conditionals can be used. Also, another new keyword is used above- "and". Our first comparison checks to see if age is less than or equal to 18 AND greater than 0. Therefore that conditional will only evaluate to true if the age value satisfies both requirements. Pretend the user input 75. The first statement evaluates, and 75 is indeed greater than 0, but it is not also less than 18, so that statement is skipped. Then, the first elif is evaluated. Age is not greater than 80, so that statement is skipped as well. Thirdly, age is definitely between 18 and 80, so the console prints "Ah, a good age to learn" and then skips the else statement altogether.

Remembering that only one statement in a decision "tree" can ever run, we can see that any elif that activates essentially runs its code block and then breaks from the decision structure. Else is used as a "catch-all" type expression in our above program. Any invalid input, such as "-1" would be picked up by else and displayed as such. Good programming form comes from catching potential user errors like this, and as an aspiring programmer you should always be expecting the user to incorrectly input values whenever the chance arises.

"And" is a comparison operator that forces both parts of an expression to be true. Another operator, "or", is used to force only one part of the expression to evaluate to true.

```
elif (age == 25 or age == 50 or age ==
75):
```
    print ("Happy quarterly birthday!")
        If we were to put this elif within
the above program (under the first if),
we would see that only one part of the
expression must be true for the whole
comparison to be true. The user's age
could be 25, 50, or 75 and the
application would say "Happy quarterly
birthday". Using "and" instead of "or"
would be impossible, because the age
cannot be 25 and 50 and 75 all at the
same time. The keywords that we use
for comparisons are helpful and greatly
useful, but if used incorrectly they can
lead to logic errors.

Example Program 2 – project2.py

```
print("Python Quiz!")

answered = 0

correct = 0

print()

print("What version of python are we
using?")

print("A: 1, B: 2, C: 3")

user_answer = input("Enter A, B, or C:
")

answered += 1
```

```python
print()

if (user_answer == "C" or user_answer
== "c"):

    correct += 1

    print ("Correct")

else:

    print ("Incorrect")

print()

print("How many 'else' statements can
be in a decision tree?")

print("A: 1, B: Infiniate, C: None")

user_answer = input("Enter A, B, or C:
")
```

```python
    answered += 1

    print()

    if (user_answer == "A" or user_answer
== "a"):

        correct += 1

        print ("Correct")

    else:

        print ("Incorrect")

    print()

    print("What does '=' do in Python?")

    print("A: Compare, B: Assign, C: Both")
```

```python
user_answer = input("Enter A, B, or C: ")

answered += 1

print()

if (user_answer == "B" or user_answer == "b"):

    correct += 1

    print ("Correct")

else:

    print ("Incorrect")

print()
```

```
print ("You got {} out of {}
correct.".format(correct, answered))


if (correct == 3):


    print ("Congratulations!  Good
score.")


elif (correct == 2):


    print ("Good work, but study hard!")


else:


    print ("Go back and read over the
section again, I'm sure you'll get it.")
```

Homework program:

- Use if statements to create a calculator program that prompts the user for two numbers and an operator.

Loops

Just as conditional statements activate if an expression evaluates to true, looping conditionals also compare values in an expression. But while if, elif, and else statements are linear in nature, other conditionals have the ability to repeatedly run blocks of code. "Loops" are conditional statements that can be run several times through the course of a program, and they allow for expanded functionality within Python programs. A "while" loop is such a conditional.

```python
answer = 0

while (answer != 2):

    answer = int(input("What is 4 / 2? "))

print ("Correct!")
```

So long as the specified condition evaluates to true, the "while" code block will continuously run. We can see a perfect example of this through the program above. We create a new variable "answer" and repeatedly compare it to 2. While answer is not equal to 2, the program will ask the user for the correct answer. Inputting something other than 2 will just loop back around to the while statement, again prompting for the correct answer. If while finally does evaluate to true (because answer equals 2) the loop will break and the program will resume by printing "Correct".

The program can be enhanced further by "nesting" conditionals. A single indentation indicates a code block set aside for our while statement, but we can go for a second level of indentation to add an additional comparison.

```
answer = 0
```

```
while (answer != 2):
```

```
answer = int(input("What is 4 / 2? "))


if (answer != 2):


    print ("Incorrect...")


print ("Correct!")
```

This program uses "nested" functions to incorporate if statements within while statements. The sheer amount of possibilities gained from this are virtually endless. Note how there are indentation levels that determine which code blocks can run within which functions. Every intended block, both 1 and 2 indent levels, will run when the while loop activates. It is a hard-to-master concept, but one that surely increases functionality.

Another common loop is the "for" loop. For is different from while in that a for loop runs through a range of numbers or a set of values instead of checking a conditional.

```
for user_variable in range (1, 5):

    print (user_variable)
```

For takes the specified variable "user_variable" and uses the supplied range. The variable will be initialized at 1, and it will be iterated every time the function loops. By observing the output we can see how this works.

```
1
2
3
4
```

User_variable is printed out, then incremented to 2. It is printed again and incremented as 3. Once more time for 4. But it reaches 5 and stops, which is why 5 does not get printed out. Because the keyword "range" was used, the for loop will always start at the first number and stop at the second. Leaving it out will have the for loop cycle through the values given.

```
for user_variable in (1, 5):

    print (user_variable)
```

For example, only "range" is left out here, but the output is very different.

```
1
5
```

Python runs the loop with the first value, 1, and then runs it with the second value, 5. We will learn that using for loops this way is especially useful for lists, dictionaries, and tuples.

Lastly, loops can be broken with the break() function. Bad programming form can lead to infinite loops, but including break() as a safeguard might save a user's computer from crashing.

Example Program 3 – project3.py

```python
print("Adding simulator")

print("Type a number to add to total, or
type blank line to stop")

line = "a"

total = 0

while (line != ""):

    line = input("")

    if (line == ""):

        break

    total += int(line)
```

```
print ("Total = {}".format(total))
```

Homework program:

- Write a program using if statements that displays a text adventure game. Offer multiple choices to the player that they can type in to select. Use while loops to check the validity of user input.

More about Variables

Lists are another data type beneficial to talk about. A list is an array of values that are grouped together into a single variable. The single variable can then be used to call upon any of the "sub variables" it contains. They are mostly used for organization and grouping purposes, and also to keep related variables in a similar place. List variables are created by initializing them.

state = "Texas"

jack_info = [8, "West Elementary", state, "A"]

print ("Jack goes to {} in {}.".format(jack_info[1], jack_info[2]))

print ("He has a {} in math, even though he's only {}.".format(jack_info[3], jack_info[0]))

The list "jack_info" contains four values because we specify four different entries between the square brackets. They are just ordinary values such as the integer 8 or the variable state, but they are grouped together for a common purpose by being placed into the list. As it is seen, entries in lists can be accessed by specifying the location of the entry in square brackets. Counting starts at 0, so the first entry of jack_info is 8, and the entry in [3] is "A". Visualize it like so:

Entry number:	0	1	2	3
Data value:	8	"West Elementary"	state	"A"

A list could be initially declared with 3 entries, and it would have the range 0-2. The number of entries is nearly infinite, and it is only limited by the computer's memory and the amount of variables the programmer fills it with.

The elements of a list can be edited as if they were individual variables. If

Jack ages a year, we only need to update the entry. Furthermore, adding a new entry to the list can be done without completely redefining every value within it. Using append(), a new entry will be created in the last

```
state = "Texas"


jack_info = [8, "West Elementary",
state, "A"]


jack_info[0] = 9


jack_info.append(22)


print ("Jack goes to {} in
{}.".format(jack_info[1], jack_info[2]))


print ("He has a {} in math, even though
he's only {}.".format(jack_info[3],
jack_info[0]))
```

print ("Lucky number is
{}".format(jack_info[4]))

The new additions to the program change the list ever so slightly to now have a new set of values.

Entry number :	0	1	2	3	4
Data value:	9	"West Elementary"	state	"A"	22

Before continuing onwards, it is worthy to note a few more features about the string data type. Strings are actually lists that contain character values. As an example, take the string "Hello, World!". Broken down as a list, it would look like this:

Entry	0	1	2	3	4	5	6	7	...
Character	H	e	l	l	o	,		W	...

And likewise, individual entries can be displayed from the string list.

```
print (user_string[0]) # would print "H"
```

```
print (user_string[7:13]) #would print
"World!"
```

Moving onwards, tuples are another data type within Python. They are declared by using parentheses instead of square brackets. Tuples are actually static lists, or lists that cannot be edited. They are used when the programmer needs to ensure a range of data cannot change.

```
jim_grades = (99, 87, 100, 99, 77)
```

```
print (jim_grades[2])
```

Notice how an entry in a tuple is still accessed using square brackets.

Dictionaries take the concept of organized variables and take it to an extreme. Just like lists and tuples, dictionaries can contain multiple values in a single variable. The difference, however, is that dictionaries organize their records through names instead of numbers. In this way, dictionaries are "unordered" lists of sorts, where any value can be called by the entry name. Declare a dictionary with curly brackets, separating out values with commas and colons.

```
pet_dict = {"Total": 2, "Dog": "Scruffy", "Cat": "Meowzer"}
```

```
print ("I have {} pets, {} and {}".format(pet_dict["Total"], pet_dict["Dog"], pet_dict["Cat"]))
```

Here, the dictionary pet_dict contains three values: "Total", "Dog", and "Cat". The entries are declared by naming the entry within quotations and then supplying a value. Those entries are called by specifying the name of the entry, such as with pet_dict["Dog"] to

176

access the value stored within. An unprecedented amount of organization is available when using dictionaries because they resemble a database in form. Likewise, they can be changed, updated, removed, or added to at any time within a program.

albums = {"Milkduds": 2, "Harold Gene": 1, "The 7750's": 3}

albums["Milkduds"] += 1 #new album!

albums["The 7750's"] = 2 #actually only had 2

albums.update({"Diamond Dozens": 1}) #found new band

del albums["Harold Gene"] #sold one away, didn't like

print ("These are the number of albums I own:")

print (albums)

The humorous example above is a simple dictionary used to store the number of albums a person has. At the beginning the dictionary has a set number of albums for each band, but the second line has the collector gaining a new Milkduds album. That line also uses a new code shortcut. Whenever "+=" is used, the code is actually expanded to be "albums["Milkduds"] = albums["Milkduds"] + 1", but much time and space is saved in the program by using the shorthand. Third line has the collector realizing they only had 2 7750's albums, so the command changes the value of the entry altogether. Next update() is introduced. It shows how an entirely new entry can be added to the dictionary. Sadly, though, Harold Gene is deleted from the dictionary because the collector sold away the album. Finally, printing the entire dictionary can be done by not specifying any entry.

A fun example, the above program actually shows how versatile dictionaries can be in gathering and storing data. Include them within your program to group variables together in an easy-to-call way.

Example Program 4 – project4.py

```python
keep_going = "a" #initialize variables
before they are used

number_grades = 0

grade_list = []

total = 0

print("Grade Average Calculator")

print()

while (keep_going != "No" and
keep_going != "no"):

    grade = int(input("Enter a test grade:
"))
```

```python
    number_grades += 1

    grade_list.append(grade)

    keep_going = input("Add more
grades? ")
print()

for x in range (0, number_grades):

    total += grade_list[x] #add up all
grades in list

print ("Average of {} tests is
{}".format(number_grades, total /
number_grades))
```

Homework program:

- Devise code for more math
  functions, such as medians and
  modes.

Functions

Every function used thus far has been built-in to Python and programmed by Python's developers. Functions are actually code shortcuts, as functions are condensed versions of code that take data as parameters, run longer blocks of code behind the scenes, and then return a result. The use of functions is to save time and code when doing commonly repeated tasks. Python retains the ability for programmers to write their own functions, and they are done like so:

```python
def happy(name):

    print ("Happy birthday to you. " * 2)

    print ("Happy birthday dear {}.".format(name))

    print ("Happy birthday to you.")
```

The "def" keyword indicates a user defined function declaration, and the name immediately following is the name of the function; we create the function happy(). Within the parentheses are the values that our function will take (only one, a variable named "name"). Just as print() must have a value, so does our happy() need one too. Then, the code associated with the function is indented. Our code simply runs through a happy birthday song, which supplying the variable "name" inside the song. This function declaration goes at the top of our python program, but it does not actually run when the program starts. To call it, we need to specifically reference the function in code.

happy("Dana")

Something interesting happens here. We call happy() by passing "Dana" as the value. "Dana" gets assigned to "name", and the function runs through. However, the variable "name" does not exist outside of the user defined function, and any attempts to call it will

result in an error. This is because
variables have scopes of operation,
which are areas in which they can be
accessed. "Name" has a variable scope
that is specific to the function, so it will
not ever be called outside of it.
Similarly, any variables declared in the
main program cannot directly be
accessed by the user defined function,
but rather they must be passed as
parameters when calling the function.
Follow along with the next exercise to
see an example for an in-depth analysis
on user defined functions (UDFs).

```
def intdiv(num_one, num_two):

    whole_answer = int(num_one /
num_two)

    remainder = num_one % num_two

    print ("{} / {} = {} with {} left

over.".format(num_one, num_two,
whole_answer, remainder))
```

```
first = int(input("Enter first number: "))

second = int(input("Enter second
number: "))

intdiv(first, second)
```

First, the UDF is declared. This code does not run automatically because it has not yet been called. The program actually starts on the fifth line. The variable "first" is declared within the main program's scope based on the user's input. So too is the variable "second". The UDF "intdiv" is invoked with first and second as the two parameters. The variables are passed as parameters so they can be transferred into the UDF. First and second are not actually leaving their scope, though, because the UDF uses the variables num_one and num_two to perform calculations.

Variables can be passed back from a UDF by using the return keyword.

```python
def exp (base, pow):

    orig_num = base

    for x in range (1, pow):

        base = base * orig_num

    return base
```

Above is a UDF that calculates the result of exponential multiplication based on two supplied values, the base and power numbers. The return keyword passes a variable back into the main program, which is how we can get around the variable's scope.

```python
answer = exp(2, 3)
```

So when we call the function like above, the answer (base) is given back as the result and assigned to the variable "answer".

Conclusively, user defined functions can save a lot of time for programs that must repeatedly call a block of code. UDFs can just contain other functions, like our Happy Birthday UDF, or they can help simplify complicated code, such as our exponential multiplication UDF. You must remember that variables are defined within a scope that they cannot leave. However, values can be passed from the main program to a UDF by supplying them as parameters, and values can return from a UDF by using the return keyword and assigning the result to a variable.

Example Program 5 – project5.py

```python
def cm_to_inch(cm):

    inch = cm * 0.39

    return inch

def inch_to_cm(inch):

    cm = inch * 2.54

    return cm

print("Inch/cm converter")

print("1: Convert cm to inch")

print("2: Convert inch to cm")
```

```python
choice = int(input("Enter a menu option: "))

while (choice != 1 and choice != 2):

    print("Invalid, try again.")

    choice = int(input("Enter a menu option: "))

if (choice == 1):

    user_input = int(input("Enter cm: "))

    print("{} cm is {} inches.".format(user_input, cm_to_inch(user_input)))

if (choice == 2):

    user_input = int(input("Enter inches: "))
```

```python
    print("{} inches is {} cm.".format(user_input, inch_to_cm(user_input)))

    print("Thank you for using the program.")
```

Homework program:

- Convert the programs you have already made to use UDFs

Classes

Classes are a feature of Python that bring it more in line with some of the more difficult programming languages. They are essentially "programs within programs" because of how many features you can put into one. Moreover, it is good programming form to use classes for organization. Object-oriented languages such as Python occasionally show their object roots through concepts like these, whereas objects contain attributes in the form "object.attribute". See the example below to understand.

```
class student:

    def __init__(self, name, grade):

        self.name = name
        self.grade = grade
        self.gpa = 0.0
```

The class that we create is called "student", and student contains its own variables. Classes give us a way to organize objects and give them personal attributes. So instead of having student1_name, student1_grade, student2_grade, etc... as different variables, they can be consolidated by belonging to a class. Within a program, the class declaration goes at the very top. Just like a UDF, it does not actually run in the main program until called.

```
student1 = student("Tim", "Freshman")
#object is student1, an attribute is
"name".
```

Our newly declared "student" class is used to create the student1 object with the attributes "Tim" and "Freshman". This would have previously taken two lines, but it is condensed considerably with classes. Classes compartmentalize the related variables of the object so that each "student" declared has the 3 properties "name", "grade", and "gpa". The second line of our class declaration contains __init__, which is a "method" (user defined function) that runs when an object in the student class is created. Init's parameters are the ones required when creating that object. Self is not actually a parameter, it just refers to "student", but "name" and "grade" are required, which is why we included them when creating "student1". Attributes of student1 can be called like so:

print (student1.name)

Which would simply print "Tim". We did not declare the GPA variable during the student1 initialization, so we can do that with an assignment statement.

student1.gpa = 4.0

Or otherwise change an attribute that already exists.

student1.grade = "Sophomore"

If we were to create another object, it would have its own set of attributes that are completely different from student1.

```
student2 = student("Mary", "Senior")
```

Where student1.grade is different from student2.grade, even though they share the same variable name. For large projects with multiple repeating variables, classes can reduce the amount of code clutter and variable names to keep track of.

Looking back to our custom class, we can expand upon it to achieve user defined functions within the class itself.

```
class student:

    def __init__(self, name, grade):

        self.name = name
```

```python
        self.grade = grade

        self.gpa = 0.0

    def record(self):

        return "Student {} is a {} with a
{}".format(self.name, self.grade,
self.gpa)

student3 = student("Lily", "Junior")

student3.gpa = 3.67

print (student3.record())
```

The __init__ stays the same, but we add a UDF definition with the name "record". It passes the parameter self (because it has to refer to the class) and returns a formatted string. In our actual main program student3 is created. Finally, we call the UDF with student3.record() (object.function). It returns our formatted string, and therefore it is printed out by print().

Special Methods

The __init__ method is actually a form of a UDF. However, methods that are surrounded by two underscores are special methods within Python, which means they run automatically at certain times. __init__ is a special method also specifically called a "constructor method". Constructor methods get called whenever an object is created, and that is why we put variable declarations within it. When student3 is created, so too are student3.name, student3.grade, and student3.gpa. Therefore, any code that is put within the __init__ block will be activated any time an object is created for the first time.

Other special methods exist, and they are called on different events.

- __del__ - called whenever an object is deleted (del). Also called destructor method.

- __str__ - called when an object is passed as a string

- __setattr__ - will run every time an attribute is set with a value

- __delattr__ - same as setattr, but only runs when an attribute is deleted

Adding in these special methods can show when they run.

```
class student:

    def __init__(self, name, grade):

        self.name = name
        self.grade = grade

        self.gpa = 0.0
```

```python
    def __str__(self):

        return "{}".format(self.name)


    def record(self):

        return "Student {} is a {} with a
{}".format(self.name, self.grade,
self.gpa)


student4 = student("Barry", "Professor")

print (student4)
```

When student4 is printed (referenced as a string), the __str__ special method takes over and returns the "name" attribute of the object. If this special method was not in there, we would not get the intended output from referencing the object.

Finally, classes are useful because we can create "class variables" within them. "Name" and "GPA" are attribute variables that are specific to each object declared, but there can also be class variables that are shared by all objects. For instance, this program will keep track of the total number of objects using a class variable.

```
class food:

    total_foods = 0

    def __init__(self, name):

        self.name = name

        self.calories = 0

        self.foodgroup = ""

        food.total_foods += 1
```

```python
    def __del__(self):

        food.total_foods -= 1

    def __str__(self):

        return "{}".format(self.name)

    def get_total():

        return food.total_foods

    def record(self):

        return "Food {0} is a {2} with {1} calories.".format(self.name, self.calories, self.foodgroup)

food1 = food("Carrot Stew")

food1.calories = 210
```

```python
food1.foodgroup = "Vegetables"

food2 = food("Buttered Toast")

food2.calories = 100

food2.foodgroup = "Grains"

print (food.get_total())

del food2

print (food.get_total())
```

As the program creates a food, 1 is added to total_foods. Then, a food object is deleted so 1 is taken away. The console prints 2, then 1 to show how our UDF can be called to check the class variable. Keeping track of the number of something is a common use for class variables, but they are highly useful for other situations as well.

Example Program 6 – project6.py

class house:

    def __init__(self, name, bedrooms, bathrooms, cost):

        self.name = name

        self.bedrooms = bedrooms

        self.bathrooms = bathrooms

        self.cost = cost

        print("House for sale!")

    def __del__(self):

        print("House off the market.")

```python
print("House for sale:")

user_input = input("What is the address
of the house? ")

user_input2 = int(input("How many
bedrooms? "))

user_input3 = int(input("How many
bathrooms? "))

user_input4 = int(input("How much
does it cost? "))

house1 = house(user_input,
user_input2, user_input3, user_input4)

print("Looking for buyers...")

for x in range (0, house1.cost):
```

```
    x += 1 #wait a while
```

```
print("Sold!")
```

```
del house1
```

Homework program:

- Use classes to make a database organization program. Users should be able to create new entries of a class and set variables, and also view them at will.

Inheritance

In your more robust and expansive programs, you might use multiple related classes. As an example, think of the program where you must categorize devices on a network. Each device type (desktop, laptop, phone, etc...) will have its own class, but you will ultimately be repeating commonly used attributes. Both desktops and laptops will have names, departments, and IP addresses, but they will also have a few distinct variables specific to them such as Wi-Fi for the laptops and graphics cards for the desktop.

Through a process called "inheritance", classes can be put into a parent/child relationship where certain parent attributes can be "inherited" by children classes. Effectively sharing attributes across classes leads to more elegant organization and less code overall.

class device:

```python
total_devices = 0

def __init__(self, name, owner):

    self.name = name

    self.owner = owner

    device.total_devices += 1

def __del__(self):

    device.total_devices -= 1

def __str__(self):

    return "{}".format(self.name)

def get_total():
```

```python
        return device.total_devices

class laptop(device):

    def __init__(self, name, owner, wifi):

        device.__init__(self, name, owner)
        self.wifi = wifi

    def __str__(self):

        return "{} is owned by {} and
connected to {}".format(self.name,
self.owner, self.wifi)

class cellular(device):

    def __init__(self, name, owner,
connection, BYOD):

        device.__init__(self, name, owner)
```

```python
        self.connection = connection

        self.BYOD = BYOD

    def __str__(self):

        return "{} is owned by {} and it uses {}.  BYOD? {}".format(self.name, self.owner, self.connection, self.BYOD)


device1 = laptop("STAFF12", "IT", "Staff-wifi")

device2 = cellular("Jack's-iDevice", "Jack", "4G LTE", "yes")

print (device1)

print (device2)

print (device.get_total())
```

In this program, the parent class "device" is created with 2 attributes – name and owner. The other classes, laptop and cellular, also contain name and owner attributes, so we set them up to inherit them from the parent class. To set a class into a parent/child relationship, the child class must pass the parent class as a parameter in the declaration. This is why "class cellular(device)" is used, because we are setting cellular to be linked to device.

Secondly, we call the device constructor method specifically within each child class constructor method. When this is done, the child class actually runs the entire parent constructor method. Name and owner are obtained this way, and also the "total_devices += 1" line gets passed as well.

Both children contain a __str__ method, even though the parent class also has one. Through a process called overwriting, if a special method is called that exists in both the parent and child, than only the child method will run. In the absence of a called method in a child, the parent will runs its method instead. This is why referencing a laptop object as a string will display laptop information, but deleting a laptop object will fall back to the parent and run its destructor method instead.

Understanding how inheritance works can provide your applications with unprecedented organization and composition. Most higher-level and advanced programs take advantage of classes and their properties to quickly devise a framework for many applications such as database tools, so learning them would undoubtedly improve your Python skills.

Example Program 7 – project7.py

```python
class house:

    def __init__(self, name, bedrooms, bathrooms):

        self.name = name

        self.bedrooms = bedrooms

        self.bathrooms = bathrooms

        self.cost = 0

        print("Living space for sale!")

    def __del__(self):

        print("Living space off the market.")
```

```python
class apartment(house):

    def __init__(self, name, bedrooms, bathrooms):

        house.__init__(self, name, bedrooms, bathrooms)

        self.montly_payment = 0

forsale1 = apartment("100 Col. Ave", 2, 2)

forsale1.montly_payment = 250
```

Homework program:

- Expand the database program that you could optionally create in the last chapter to include inheritance.

Modules

Every bit of functionality that we have used so far is built-in to Python already. Python is an expansive language, but additional features can be added to Python easily through modules. Those familiar with C can relate modules to "h" files and preprocessor statements. Modules do much the same thing, they are included in order to add new functions and commands to Python.

To add a new module, we only need to include one statement at the top of our program.

```
import math
```

So in this line, we import the "math" module, which opens up a slew of new functions for us to use.

```
import math

print (math.sin(3))
```

```
answer = math.sqrt(16)

print (answer)

print (math.gcd(100, 125))
```

In particular, sqrt(), sin(), and gcd() are three examples you can notice above. Every module has a defined purpose, and math's is to provide advanced mathematical functions. Here is a list of the most important ones.

- math.sqrt() – square root of number

- math.sin() – sine of number

- math.cos() – cosine of number

- math.tan() – tangent of number

- math.log() – two parameters, log and base

- math.pi – 3.14159

- math.e – 2.71828

Those needing to use complicated functions such as the ones above only need to "import math" at the top of the program.

Other specialized modules exist as well, such as datetime. Datetime is a module that provides time-keeping functions.
import datetime

current_time = datetime.datetime.now()

print (current_time.hour)

```
print (current_time.minute)
```

```
print (current_time.second)
```

Other functions provided through datetime include:

- year
- month
- day

Or os, a module that unlocks operating system functions for altering files. Here is a small program for creating a new folder and then making it the active directory.

```
import os
```

```
os.mkdir("folder") #make folder
```

os.chdir("folder") #go into folder

os.chdir("..") #up one directory

More functions available to os are listed.

- os.rmdir() – delete specified folder

- os.remove() – delete specified file

- os.path.exists() – checks to see if specified file exists

- os.rename() – renames specified file to second parameter supplied

And other highly useful modules, such as random, statistics, and pip exist that can give new features to your Python applications that were not previously possible. Python also has support for downloading and using user-created modules, but that is an advanced concept not covered here.

Example Program 8 – project8.py

```python
import random

print ("Fortune telling...")

rng = random.randrange(1, 7)

if (rng == 1):

    print("You will soon come into money.")

elif (rng == 2):

    print("Consider buying stocks.")

elif (rng == 3):
```

```python
    print("Look both ways before
crossing.")

elif (rng == 4):

    print("Call your relatives...")

elif (rng == 5):

    print("You will get a phone call.")
else:

    print("Future cloudy... Try again.")
```

Homework project:

- Create a "sampler" program that shows off various Python module features.

Common Errors

Because many programmers choose Python as their first language to learn, they often succumb to a few common errors. If your applications are not functioning correctly, or if you are looking for a few of the best programming practices, than this section will help you. When code is run through Python, it may stop and return an error to you. By reading the error you can learn which line the error comes from, and usually Python will point (^) to the exact character that is wrong. Use the information that is given to you to understand your error and rectify the situation.

Not specifying the correct parameters is a common newbie mistake. When putting values between the parentheses for a function, you must pay close attention to what kind of data it expects. Some functions require only integers, and some have 2 or more parameters to enter. When in doubt, consult the Python documentation page for the specific function you are working with. Advanced IDEs, such as Atom and Eclipse often are programmed to display an example parameter list as you are typing out a function, and you can follow along with the example to know what each parameter is expecting.

Sometimes we forget to convert user input to an integer. If we are prompting a user for numerical input, we must surround input() with int() for float(). Failure to do this will pass the input as a string, which will likely return an error.

When comparing two values, Python requires the programmer to use the double equal sign (==). When assigning a value, you must use the single equal sign (=). Using an inappropriate sign for any occasion will always return a syntax error.

After every comparison statement and loop (such as if, elif, else, for, while, def, and class) there is a colon (:). This colon denotes that the next line should be indented, and thus all indented lines will fall within the function's scope. Failure to place a colon returns a syntax error.

Strings and functions are usually surrounded by a pair of characters. Functions use parentheses, while strings use quotations to indicate where their boundaries are. If you ever forget to supply the closing character, Python will surely return an error.

Beginners will often try to use functions that are not in Python by default without including the correct module. Trying to call an advanced math function, or editing a file directory is not possible with regular Python. Always place the import commands for modules you will use at the top of the program, or the application will simply not run.

Indentations are required in Python. Those coming from other programming languages will likely forget this and indent in their own personal style. This will break mostly all Python programs, because the interpreter expects a certain formatting standard. An error will be returned every time that indentations are incorrect. Pay close attention to your indentation levels or risk your program failing to logic and syntax errors.

Programming languages demand perfect syntax at all times. Because of this, even a spelling error can be disastrous for our applications. Besides indentation problems and misspelled functions, giving the wrong variable name or accidentally calling the wrong function can make your program fail outright or perform unexpectedly. When coding, double check over your scripts to ensure no characters are out of place. Test your code after each implementation so you know that when an error occurs it should be coming from a new addition. Sometimes there is an error or bug in the code and it just cannot be rectified after reviewing the code. Programmers must "debug" their code by following it line-by-line at this point, "tracing" the path that the interpreter takes as it runs the program.

Some IDE's have tools for debugging, such as "breakpoints" or "line stops" that allow you to run each line at the click of a button. Taking the program slow like that can reveal the source of the issue most of the time, but it takes a keen eye and a dedicated troubleshooter to fix code.

Many programmers consider it unnecessary, but commenting your scripts is an essential part of coding. Failure to do so is an extremely common beginner mistake that many first time programmers fall for. Once you master the art of Python and begin programming in a company with other coders, there might be multiple people working on the same script. Even the cleanest code is confusing to look at for the first time, but comments help to demystify the complex characters. Moreover, coming back to an old script of yours from weeks past can feel like reading a foreign language- comments help you to quickly get back to coding. Many programmers put a comment as the top line of their program with a brief description of what the script does, when it was written, and any contributors to it. That way the next time you are quickly looking through files trying to find a certain program, the comments can help you understand what is inside without actually running or deciphering the code.

The final common mistake that runs rampant in Python newbies is variable naming. If it has not already been brought to light in your experimentation, there are just certain names that you cannot name your variables. "Reserved" words such as class, break, print, and, or, while, etc... are keywords that cannot be used for a variable name. If Python detects their use a syntax error will occur. Besides errors, though, programmers often use bad form when naming their variables. Avoid ambiguous and simple variable names such as "number" or "var1" in favor of descriptive one such as "user_input" or "totalNumberOfDogs". These variables explain their use at a glance, so a verbose programmer will never misuse a variable or have to check what its intent is. Python programmers typically use the underscore method to name their variables (grade_average, dog_1), but camelCase is acceptable as well (userInput, multAnswer). No matter which method is used, a skillful programmer will always make the name descriptive.

Conclusion

Thank you again for downloading this beginner's guide to Python. Now that you have finished the text, you have a basic knowledge of how Python works, and you should be able to write your own programs. You can further increase your knowledge by attempting to create larger and more complicated programs, or you can study modules and learn new functions. If you have enjoyed the book, rate and leave a review on Amazon so more high quality books can be produced.

Related Titles

Hacking University: Freshman Edition Essential Beginner's Guide on How to Become an Amateur Hacker

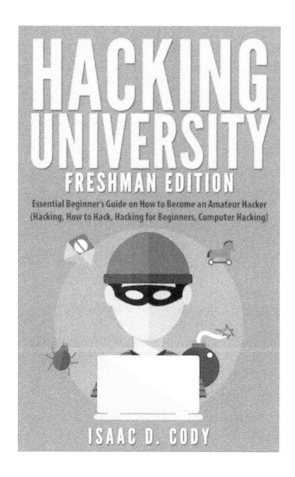

Hacking University: Sophomore Edition. Essential Guide to Take Your Hacking Skills to the Next Level. Hacking Mobile Devices, Tablets, Game Consoles, and Apps

Hacking University: Junior Edition.
Learn Python Computer Programming
From Scratch. Become a Python Zero to
Hero. The Ultimate Beginners Guide in
Mastering the Python Language

Hacking University: Senior Edition
Linux. Optimal Beginner's Guide To
Precisely Learn And Conquer The Linux
Operating System. A Complete Step By
Step Guide In How Linux Command
Line Works

Hacking University: Graduation Edition.
4 Manuscripts (Computer, Mobile,
Python, & Linux). Hacking Computers,
Mobile Devices, Apps, Game Consoles
and Learn Python & Linux

Data Analytics: Practical Data Analysis and Statistical Guide to Transform and Evolve Any Business, Leveraging the power of Data Analytics, Data Science, and Predictive Analytics for Beginners

C++: Learn C++ Like a Boss. A Beginners Guide in Coding Programming And Dominating C++. Novice to Expert Guide To Learn and Master C++ Fast

About the Author

Isaac D. Cody is a proud, savvy, and ethical hacker from New York City. Currently, Isaac now works for a mid-size Informational Technology Firm in the heart of NYC. He aspires to work for the United States government as a security hacker, but also loves teaching others about the future of technology. Isaac firmly believes that the future will heavily rely computer "geeks" for both security and the successes of companies and future jobs alike. In his spare time, he loves to analyze and scrutinize everything about the game of basketball.